T H E
I-Don't-Eat

(BUT-I-CAN'T-LOSE)

Weight Loss Program

THE
I-Don't-Eat

(BUT-I-CAN'T-LOSE)

Weight Loss Program

STEVEN JONAS, M.D., M.P.H.
and
VIRGINIA ARONSON, R.D., M.S.

RAWSON ASSOCIATES
NEW YORK

Rawson Associates
Macmillan Publishing Company
866 Third Avenue, New York, N.Y. 10022
Collier Macmillan Canada, Inc.

Library of Congress Cataloging-in-Publication Data

Jonas, Steven.
    The I don't eat (but I can't lose) weight-loss
program.

    Includes index.
    1. Obesity—Popular works.   2. Reducing—Popular
works.   I. Aronson, Virginia.   II. Title.
RC628.J63   1989   613.2'5   88-61266
ISBN 0-89256-343-5

Macmillan books are available at special discounts for bulk purchases for sales promotions, premiums, fund-raising, or educational use.
For details, contact:

    Special Sales Director
    Macmillan Publishing Company
    866 Third Avenue
    New York, N.Y. 10022

Packaged by Rapid Transcript, a division of March Tenth, Inc.

Designed by Stanley S. Drate/Folio Graphics Company, Inc.

Illustrations by Jackie Aher

10 9 8 7 6 5 4 3 2 1

Printed in the United States of America

To the memory of my maternal grandfather, Jacob Kyzor,
who first introduced me to the pleasures of walking

Acknowledgments

I would like to thank my agent, Harvey Klinger, for his patience and good humor in seeing this project through to completion. He is a good friend.

I thank my department chairman, Dr. Andre Varma, of the Department of Community and Preventive Medicine, School of Medicine, State University of New York at Stony Brook, for his support.

—STEVEN JONAS

Many thanks go to my agent, Connie Clausen, for her demonstrated belief in the value of this project and for her selection of the best publisher for it, Eleanor Rawson.

—VIRGINIA ARONSON

Contents

Before You Begin This Book

*I*n the spring of 1980, I was an overweight, overfat, totally sedentary, stereotypical forty-three-year-old college professor. At the time, I considered myself healthy—not fit, not in tiptop shape, but certainly not *unhealthy*. I didn't smoke cigarettes, never had. I rarely drank alcohol. My blood pressure was actually lower than average, and all blood tests yielded normal results. I wasn't worried that I was at imminent risk for heart attack or stroke, and I conscientiously wore my seatbelt while driving—just to be on the safe side. I sometimes caught an occasional cold or flu but rarely missed more than a day of work due to illness. So I *thought* that I was in pretty good shape.

However, most of the time, I avoided stepping onto the bathroom scales because the numbers would depress me. I wasn't *seriously* overweight, not enough to concern my physician. Even so, the scales reflected what I felt inside: I *was* overweight. But I didn't do anything about it.

My diet was another aspect of my life back then that needed attention. I knew that I was consuming way too much fat, that my nighttime binges were unbalanced, that skipping breakfast daily and indulging in weekly ice cream pig-outs were unwise. Deep inside I felt that I needed to change my relationship with food. But I didn't do a thing.

I had finally realized that I really needed to do some sort of regular exercise. As a physician specializing in health-oriented medicine, I had just begun working as a consultant to the health-oriented medical education program at the Texas College of Osteopathic Medicine in Fort Worth. My colleagues there were all enthusiastic joggers, bicyclists, and weight lifters. I was conspicuous by my absence in the gym. So I started thinking about becoming a jogger myself. I thought about it all throughout that spring, right through the summer, and into the fall. But I did nothing.

As I write this book, it is the fall of 1988, some eight years later. I have recently completed my second Ironman triathlon. This endurance event begins with a 2.4-mile ocean swim, followed by a 112-mile bike race, and concludes with a full 26.2-mile marathon run. This time, I PaceWalked the entire marathon leg of the course. (*PaceWalking* is my own term for brisk striding, one of the best forms of exercise for people of all ages and sizes.) I wanted to compare my finishing time and my level of fatigue with my first Ironman event, in which I had jogged for much of the marathon course.

As of this writing, I have completed over twenty triathlons of various lengths, including the two Ironman events. I have PaceWalked two marathons and run four others, plus I've completed five half marathons, several biathlons (in which you bike and run), and a number of road races of ten kilometers or less. I'm not a professional athlete. I'm not even a "serious" athlete, because I never compete to win, only to finish and to enjoy myself. But I am indeed an athlete. And I'm physically fit, in tiptop shape, and *no longer overweight*.

What happened? How did I transform myself from an over-stuffed couch potato into a trim triathlete? How did I become a thinner, fitter version of my formerly fat self? Was this a fluke, some sort of magic trick, a miracle—*or can anyone do what I did?* Even if you don't plan on competing in races or attempting to become an athlete, I have good news for you. In fact, I have good news for *anyone* who wants to make some lifestyle changes, for all who need to alter (poor) eating and (non)exercising habits: *You can do it!* How? By following the step-by-step program provided in this book. It worked for me, and it will work for you, too.

GETTING OUT OF THE DIET TRAP

As you'll discover when you read the chapters that follow, I made slow, gradual, careful changes in my eating and exercise patterns. My transformation did not occur overnight, but I *did* change my body and my life—safely and permanently. I can state without hesitation that *I will never again go on a low-calorie diet, keep count of calories, or starve myself* in attempts to lose weight. Dieting is unhealthy, depressing, and ultimately self-defeating. Diets don't work, not if you want to shed excess body fat safely and permanently. Instead, I have discovered the effective way to trim down and tone up, the *ideal* way. And I will now share my step-by-step program, the IDEAL (that is, the *I Don't Eat A Lot*) Weight-Loss Program with *you*.

The program is ideal because it is not a fad diet or a crash weight-loss plan. It is based on the scientifically and medically sound method to eat well *and* lose weight. It is nutritionally complete, psychologically satisfying, and can be followed healthfully for the rest of your life. There are no calories to be counted, no menu plans to abide by, no gimmicks or supplements that must be purchased. And there is no deadline by which you must be transformed into a "perfect" specimen. The goal of ultra-thinness encouraged by media images of stereotyped physical perfection is in fact unrealistic, ultimately leading to feelings of defeat, depression, and disappointment. Safe, sensible weight loss, however, *will* improve your health, enhance your fitness, and make you look and feel better—far more satisfying goals for you to strive for *and attain*.

The IDEAL program helps you to set realistic and reasonable goals. The plans you design are personal and flexible, the changes you make are gradual, and the results are lifelong. This program does not claim to be the last diet you will ever go on—and off— because it is not just another diet. Once you adopt the IDEAL Eating and Exercise Plans, *you won't need to diet, count calories, or starve yourself ever again*.

The program set out in this book is specially designed to help the millions of chronic dieters who have tried every weight-loss regimen to cross their paths, usually quitting in hungry frustration and always regaining any weight lost—plus some additional poundage. *It is for people who really don't eat a lot but still can't lose.* This was the ideal weight-loss program for me, and it can prove ideal for you, too.

If diets don't do the job for you, it is probably because you have a metabolic condition I call Low-Calorie Overweight or Diet-Induced Overweight, in which the body becomes highly efficient at saving energy. For the person with this condition, *low-calorie diets do not lead to weight loss because the body is able to adapt* to the restriction. Most people who diet repeatedly eventually develop Diet-Induced Overweight. Fad diets and chronic calorie cutting trigger, then aggravate the condition. The IDEAL Weight-Loss Program, however, enables you to *take control.*

If you do not have Low-Calorie Overweight (there is a self-diagnosis questionnaire included in chapter 2), the program can still work for you. The IDEAL Exercise Plan will help you to become physically active, fit, and trim without strain and pain. Because the focus of the exercise plan is on a sport that I call PaceWalking, just about *everyone can participate.* And the guideline for measuring your success is your participation, not your performance. All you have to do is walk—regularly, consistently, briskly. You will shed fat, build muscle, and look better. And you'll notice results right away: You will immediately feel better about yourself.

If you do have Diet-Induced Overweight, the IDEAL Weight-Loss Program will help you to balance your diet and increase your activity levels, gradually phasing out excess fats and adding in exercise so that you can eat more healthfully, *eat more food, and still lose weight.* Low-calorie and fad diets are ineffective for you and will only contribute further to your condition. Instead of giving up foods, give up dieting! Regular exercise and healthful eating are the only ways you can finally take control of your body— and stay in control for good.

Whether you are currently a chronic dieter, an overeater, or a sedentary person with a high fat intake (you will learn how to determine and adjust the fat content of your daily diet in Section III), the IDEAL Weight-Loss Program can help you. This program is for anyone who wants to get in shape—and stay that way for life.

GETTING PSYCHED TO CHANGE

The 1980s has been an era marked by unprecedented interest in self-help and self-improvement. The fitness boom is an impressive example of our society's movement toward self-change—not just for the sake of appearance, but for physical and emotional well-being. The blossoming of the so-called New Age is a more recent outgrowth of our personal and social drive toward change, toward making ourselves better and the world a better place to live. Progress in the New Age begins with balancing ourselves—physically, emotionally, and spiritually—by changing ourselves.

But it's not easy to begin to make changes, even on the smallest scale.

It took me a long time to begin to change my eating habits. Until I was able to change my self-image from fat to fit, I remained overweight, out of shape, disharmonious. I had to dig deep down inside and tap into the motivation, the drive, the emotional and spiritual desire that lay within. For many years, I was afraid to do just that.

Fear can serve as a major barrier to personal success. In my case, I was afraid that I *couldn't* become athletic, that I would appear clumsy and uncoordinated. In my own mind, I was a physician, a scientist, a professor—not an athlete. My self-image was of an overweight klutz, not a potentially svelte athlete. So I allowed all my fears of the unknown, my perennial insecurities and warped self-appraisals to block my personal progress. I was also afraid that adopting a healthful eating pattern would mean that I would be forced to give up all of my favorite foods. The idea of eliminating hot fudge sundaes forever was too depressing. I didn't want to attempt to improve my diet . . . and then *fail*. So I let my fear of failure stand in the way of my personal growth. I barricaded myself in my own inner prison. And I stayed stuck in my own mind trap for a long time, dissatisfied with the status quo yet fearful of change.

Finally, one memorable day in October of 1980, I found the key to my inner prison and *I let myself out*. I'm a free man now, in control of my life and myself. I like my life much better this way, and I like myself a lot more, too. I'm not perfect, but I no longer aspire to be. I exercise regularly and I love doing it. But some days I don't exercise, and that's okay, too—nobody's perfect. I eat well-balanced, low-fat meals and snacks, and I truly enjoy the food I choose to eat. But sometimes I splurge on a fancy restaurant meal or an occasional hot fudge sundae. And this is okay, too. Nobody's perfect. I'm not perfect, but I'm no longer overweight. I'm now trim and fit. I feel so much better, healthy inside and out. And this feels great!

That's why I want to share the IDEAL Weight-Loss Program with you. This program can do the same for you. Make the choice to take control of your body and your life. The IDEAL Weight-Loss Program will give you the step-by-step guidelines to help you do just that.

℞: MEDICAL WARNING

This book is not intended to be used as a substitute for your physician's advice. If you have a serious medical condition such as heart disease, high blood pressure, diabetes, or other chronic disease, it is essential to follow the IDEAL Weight-Loss Program only *under your doctor's supervision.* This is also advisable if you are over the age of fifty or more than fifty pounds overweight.

Because the IDEAL Exercise Plan is a *walking program,* and since the IDEAL Eating Plan is *not a low-calorie diet* but is based on well-balanced low-fat nutrition, the IDEAL Weight-Loss Program is medically sound. It is indeed ideal for just about everyone, fit or fat.

STEVEN JONAS, M.D., M.P.H.
Fall 1988

I Don't Eat a Lot— So Why Don't I Lose?

1

Steve's Success Story: How I Changed Myself for Good

*A*t age forty-three, I had to break down and admit that years of sedentary living and too much rich food had gradually caught up with me, forming a small tire around my middle. It can happen to the best of us! But when I realized that *I* was out of shape, I was upset with myself. Here I was, a physician and a professor of preventive medicine, and I had generous "love handles" on my waistline! I was only preaching wellness, not practicing it myself.

THE MOMENT OF TRUTH

I could have lost weight, started jogging, and reformed my dietary habits out of guilt or shame. But I didn't have a *positive* reason to make changes in my life. And it's only positive motivators that really work. So I didn't start exercising and I continued to overeat; meanwhile the war within me raged on.

And then it happened. It was 8:15 on a Tuesday morning, October 21, 1980. I was attending a medical conference at the convention center in Detroit, on my way to a workshop on an upper floor. The convention center floors are connected by ramps, and I had to walk up one to get to the meeting room. By the time I reached the top, only one flight up, I was huffing and puffing. I could hear my heavy breathing and feel my heart pounding in my chest. My body was behaving as if I had pushed it to its physical limits—which I had—simply by walking slowly up a slight incline!

I realized at last that it was time to start on a program. My body was telling me what my mind could no longer deny: I was fat and unfit, and it was time for me to deal with my unhealthy condition. I was finally ready, willing, and able to do so. I *wanted* to get fit for my own sake.

PERSONAL DISCOVERY

Even as a child, I was never very good at sports. I couldn't by any stretch of the imagination be considered fast, and my eye-hand coordination was poor. So I stayed away from athletics and buried myself in my studies. While in medical school, I discovered the excitement of downhill skiing. I loved it! And a dozen years later, I fell in love with sailing. But I skied and sailed in seasonal spurts and continued to regard myself as unathletic.

So I was amazed to find out at age forty-three that I actually had an athlete within, just waiting to be let out. For over four decades, I had not allowed myself to be all that I was capable of *physically*. I had no idea that I would one day be able to jog for twenty minutes, never mind complete a triathlon spanning over sixteen hours!

I decided to start with small steps. I planned to succeed, so I didn't set myself up for failure. And I wanted to enjoy the process, so I was determined to avoid pain, boredom, overexertion, and burn-out. I decided to become a three-times-a-week-for-twenty-minutes jogger.

As soon as I returned home from the convention in Detroit, I drew up an exercise plan. Three times a week I would go up to the local high school track. I began slowly, carefully, and easily, alternating two minutes of brisk walking with two minutes of slow jogging. And by the end of the first month, I could jog for a full twenty minutes without stopping.

By the following spring, I was jogging from thirty-five to forty minutes four or five times a week. But right from the beginning, even as I was alternating walking and jogging, *I liked how exercise made me feel.* It made me feel stronger, more powerful, in control of my body and my life. And it still does.

FROM JOGGER TO IRONMAN

As I achieved each of my personal exercise goals, I set new ones. One year after I began jogging, I purchased my first ten-speed bicycle. I drew up a new draft of my exercise plan, substituting thirty-minute bike rides for two of the forty-minute runs. By alternating activities, I worked out different sets of muscles, preventing overuse injuries. It also kept my interest level piqued.

The following spring, I ran my first road race, a five-mile course. My goal was to complete the course in fifty minutes, that is, at my usual pace of ten-minute miles. I crossed the finish line in forty-three minutes. Of course, I didn't win any trophies (the winning time was less than half my own), but that had not been my goal. I had successfully completed a race and had actually exceeded my personal goal, a discovery that meant far more to me than a plaque or blue ribbon. I felt like a real athlete, and I promptly set some new athletic goals.

Six months later I ran my first ten-kilometer race. Then I joined a local running club that held regular group workouts every Sunday. Through the club, I met another novice runner who had a goal I hadn't yet considered: running a marathon. Twenty-six miles nonstop. It sounded crazy! But somehow the idea of setting manageable intermediate goals and working toward a big goal like a marathon captured my interest, so I set up a training program for it.

In 1983, I completed a twenty-mile race, following that up at the end of the year with a full-scale marathon in Dallas. The best part of the marathon was that I was running with students and staff members from the Texas College of Osteopathic Medicine, the folks who had first inspired me to exercise three years earlier!

In the meantime, I had discovered triathlons. I hadn't swum for any distance since childhood, but I remembered the strokes and I had built up plenty of stamina. As with cycling and running, I was slow but steady. I didn't set out to win any triathlons. I just wanted to complete one—and see if I enjoyed the event.

I entered my first triathlon in the fall of 1983. I not only enjoyed the event (a "short-course" triathlon with a 1.5-mile swim, 25-mile bike ride, and 10-mile run), I got hooked! Two years later, after completing nearly a dozen triathlons of varying lengths, I entered the Bud Light Endurance Triathlon on Cape Cod. It took me sixteen hours and forty-two minutes to complete the 2.4-mile swim, 112-mile bike ride, and 26.2-mile run—sixteen hours longer than it took me to complete my first race a little over three years earlier. But I did it and felt great at the end!

THAT LEAN LOOK

Along the road to discovering the athlete within, I lost fifteen pounds of body fat and three inches of "love handles" from my waistline. My body fat percentage dropped from 26 to 18 (see chart on page 37). Yet *I did not diet, not even for a day*. I had gradually improved my eating habits but didn't restrict my caloric intake or forbid myself food favorites. Instead of counting calories, I had begun to regard food as fuel. Eventually, eating well felt so good that I decided to provide my body with the best fuel for functioning optimally *all the time*.

By treating my body with respect, I found a well of self-respect within. I was physically, psychologically, and spiritually uplifted, and it felt great! I decided that I deserve to feel this good *every* day—for the rest of my life.

You may not choose to run races, enter triathlons, or compete in an Ironman endurance event, but your own transformation can be equally dramatic. With the IDEAL Weight-Loss Program, there is nothing to stop you from shedding fat and getting fit. Don't wait for years like I did! Do it now, *do it for you*. You, too, deserve to look and feel great. And I'm going to show you how to do it. Let's begin!

2

Getting Out of the Diet Trap: Why Dieters Get Stuck and How You Can Come Unstuck

When I was in medical school, physiology coursework taught me that too many calories taken in (as food) and too few calories expended (in physical activity) resulted in weight gain. To induce weight loss, the balance had to be reversed. "If your overweight patients tell you that they aren't overeating, they're lying," we were taught.

Guess what? The caloric balance theory was *wrong!* My teachers in medical school were *wrong!* So for many years, my own understanding of calories and weight control was *wrong.* I thought that calories were important, that counting calories was important. They aren't, and it isn't. The real bottom line in weight control is *the pace at which the body functions.*

YOUR PERSONAL PACE

The body, even at rest, is at work. The heart is constantly beating, the digestive organs are handling food and fluids, the body's internal temperature is regulating itself. To keep all systems functioning, the body requires energy. And when muscles are in action, when the body is moving, more energy is needed. The functioning of the body's systems is known as METABOLISM. The energy for metabolism is supplied by food, which is converted into the body's fuel, GLUCOSE. The amount of energy supplied by food and used in metabolism is measured in CALORIES. And the speed at which all this works is your METABOLIC RATE.

Your metabolic rate is determined by your body build, sex, age, and genetic makeup. Some of us are born with slower than normal metabolic rates and tend to gain weight easily. Others are born with faster than normal metabolic rates, so tend to be on the slim side, if not downright skinny. Fatter folk usually envy their naturally thin peers, those who seem able to eat absolutely anything without gaining a pound. Bigger, more muscular people usually have higher metabolic rates, and males typically enjoy speedier metabolic rates than females. The metabolic rate also tends to slow down with age, beginning gradually in the late twenties and dropping more markedly after the fifth decade of life.

Would you like to be able to take control of your metabolic rate? Would you like to be able to speed up a sluggish metabolism, emulating those naturally thin folks you now envy? You can do just that and, unless you are one of the very rare individuals with a metabolic disorder requiring medication, *you can rev up your metabolism simply by making some lifestyle changes*.

FAT FROM DIETING

The two major causes of slowed metabolism are sedentary living habits and low-calorie dieting. And *these are two factors you can control*. With regular exercise and low-fat nutrition, your metabolic rate can be boosted—you'll build muscle and shed fat. In fact, by exercising regularly and eating right, you may be able to minimize or delay the age-related downward drop of your metabolic rate. Active women can even overcome the metabolic sex bias. BUT YOU HAVE TO EXERCISE AND YOU MUST STOP DIET-ING. Otherwise, your metabolic rate will remain slower than nor-mal, and you will remain fatter than you'd like to be.

Exercise burns calories directly and also builds muscles, which require more energy to function than does body fat, thereby in-creasing the body's need for fuel. Exercise perks up the metabolic rate during *and for hours after* physical activity, further increasing the need for fuel. And exercise can reset a sluggish metabolic rate, permanently increasing the body's fuel needs. If you exercise, you can eat *more* food—low-fat, nutrient-rich food—to supply the extra fuel your active body needs.

But, you ask, if I want to lose weight, shouldn't I exercise and go on a *low-calorie* diet? No! The low-calorie diet will actually sabo-tage the metabolism-boosting effects of regular exercise. Studies show that physically active individuals with restricted caloric in-takes have slowed metabolisms, *as sluggish as if they weren't even exercising!* The body adapts to the reduced caloric/fuel intake as if you were in danger of starving and slows down the function of bodily systems in order to protect itself. This is known as the "starvation response," and it occurs whenever caloric intakes are inadequate—with or without exercise. Some researchers believe that the starvation response may be even more severe in those who exercise and follow a low-calorie diet. But even if you are seden-tary, an inadequate caloric intake will trigger the starvation re-sponse, resulting in a slowed metabolic rate, easy fat gain, and the inability to lose weight *even though you don't eat a lot.* Obviously, low-calorie diets—especially for physically active individuals—are counterproductive if you are attempting to shed excess body fat. Dieting, counting calories, self-starvation—with or without exer-cise—will cause rather than cure a weight problem.

FAD DIETS

BE SLEEK IN A WEEK! LOSE FAT FAST!
MELT OFF POUNDS—AS YOU SLEEP!

Do you try out the latest diet, hot off the press—one after the other? Have you been dieting on and off for years? If so, you are not alone. Millions of your fellow Americans are currently attempting a weight-loss diet. Most will fail. And it won't be their fault. Most people are unaware that *low-calorie diets lead to weight gain.*

Complete the Self-Evaluation on Fad Diets below to help refresh your memory about your dieting history. For this self-evaluation and the rest of the activities in this book, use a personal diary that you can write in and carry with you. You might want to buy a small spiral-bound notebook that will easily fit into a purse, briefcase, or knapsack. Or, if you want to make a copy of each of the self-evaluations and charts included in this book, you might want to purchase a looseleaf notebook the same size as the book. That way, you can photocopy what you need to keep on hand and punch holes in the materials to insert into your personal notebook. This will be your IDEAL Log, one of the most helpful tools in making lifestyle changes.

In completing the following self-evaluation, be as accurate as you can, and be honest. This will help you to determine whether your dieting habits have led you to develop Diet-Induced Overweight. And if you find that dieting did get you into trouble, *don't worry.* This program can bail you out.

SELF-EVALUATION ON FAD DIETS

Which of the popular diets listed below have you tried? How long did you follow each of these diets? Did you lose weight? If so, did you keep it off? For how long? Describe your dieting history in your IDEAL Log, using the list to help jog your memory. If there are any other diets you have undertaken—with or without a doctor's supervision—describe these in your log as well.

Popular Diets

- Starvation diet/modified fast
- Liquid diet/juice fast
- Monofood diet (e.g., brown rice and tea, or cottage cheese only)
- Rice diet
- Beverly Hills diet
- U.S. Air Force diet
- I Love New York diet
- Scarsdale diet
- Southampton diet
- Immune Power diet
- High-protein diet
- Liquid protein diet

- Fruitarian diet (fruit only)
- Grapefruit diet
- Fit for Life diet
- Low-carbohydrate diet
- Dr. Atkins' diet
- Dr. Stillman's diet
- U.S. Ski Team diet
- Last Chance diet
- Cambridge diet
- Herbalife diet
- Nutri-systems diet
- Weight Loss Center diet
- Rotation diet
- Low-calorie diet

DIET-INDUCED, LOW-CALORIE OVERWEIGHT

If you indicated in your self-evaluation that you have attempted *more than one fad diet,* you probably now suffer from Diet-Induced Overweight. A complete questionnaire for self-diagnosis is provided a few pages further on. But the quickest method for self-analysis is to ask yourself whether the first part of the title of this book describes you: I DON'T EAT (BUT I CAN'T LOSE). If you sometimes starve yourself but still are above normal in body fat content, YOU HAVE LOW-CALORIE OVERWEIGHT.

Don't feel guilty, depressed, or defeated. You didn't know that dieting causes Low-Calorie Overweight. *It's not your fault.* And this is true for a significant percentage of the overweight American public. You are not alone.

Fortunately, Diet-Induced Overweight is treatable—BUT NOT WITH LOW-CALORIE DIETS. Diets don't work for you. They may have made you fat in the first place, and will only make you even fatter.

A WORD ABOUT FAT

Do you flinch at the words *fat* and *obese?* It is time to set these terms straight. Don't faint, just take a look at the following *scientific* definitions for these often misunderstood terms:

- *Overweight*—body weight above the "desirable" range due to disproportionate lean muscle tissue, bones, fluids, and/or fat stores
- *Obese*—body weight 15 percent or more above the "desirable" range due to excess fat
- *Fat*—stored energy in the body, also known as adipose tissue

Thus, one can have too much body fat without being over-*weight!* This often occurs in sedentary people who don't overeat. If one is *obese*, both body fat and body weight are markedly elevated. Then there are overweight people who are *not* overfat, such as muscular football players and pregnant women. These people don't need to lose weight.

WAIST-HIP MEASUREMENT AND HEALTHY WEIGHT

The following waist-hip measurement guidelines and the Body Mass Index Chart will help you determine whether you need to lose excess weight and fat. If you are overweight but not overfat, you may already be at the weight that is healthy for *you*. If so, you can stop worrying about the numbers on the bathroom scales. (More on the tyranny of the scales later.)

First, use a tape measure to determine your *Waist-Hip Ratio:*

- Look in a full-length mirror to find the right spots.
- Measure your waist circumference at the level of your navel.
- Measure your hip circumference at the *widest* point.
- Do not pull the tape measure so tightly that your results are underestimated.
- Divide the width of your waist by the width of your hips to determine your *Waist-Hip Ratio.*

For men, a Waist-Hip Ratio of more than one (1.0) indicates the need to lose body weight/fat. For women, a ratio greater than 0.8 means body weight/fat loss is required.

Next, use a ruler and the chart that follows to determine your Body Mass Index (BMI):

- Place the edge of the ruler so it lines up your height (in inches, at the left of the chart) with your weight (in pounds, on the right of the chart).
- Where the ruler crosses on the scaled line in the middle indicates your weight situation.
- If the ruler does not pass through the grid, but lines up above the grid, you then fall into the overweight category. If it lines up below the grid, you fall into the underweight category.
- To determine your healthy weight range, slide the ruler down

BODY MASS INDEX

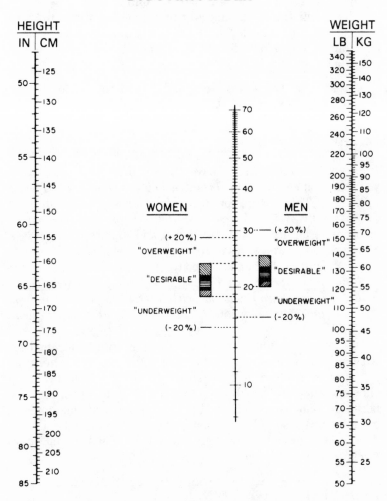

Source: Anthony E. Thomas, Ph.D., David A. McKay, M.D., and Michael B. Cutlip, Ph.D. "A Nomograph Method for Assessing Body Weight." *The American Journal of Clinical Nutrition*, 29:303, 1976. Reprinted by permission.

until it falls within the "desirable" weights range, and note the weights given in the right-hand column.
- Take your frame into account by examining where the ruler falls in the shaded block—the top of the block is for large frames, the middle for medium frames, and the bottom for small frames.

Record your *Waist-Hip Ratio,* BMI, and "desirable" healthy weight range in your IDEAL Log for future reference.

HAZARDOUS WAIST

Recent scientific studies have shown that *where* you deposit your extra fat can be as important as *how much* excess you've got in storage. This is true for weight-loss purposes as well as for overall health. Excess upper body fat is associated with an increased risk for heart disease, diabetes, and other serious illnesses. However, on a weight-loss program, the upper-area fat can be reduced more easily than lower body fat stores. Thus, *fat stored in the tummy area is more of a health threat but, fortunately, easier to lose. Fat deposited below the beltline—that is, the flab on hips, buttocks, and thighs—is not a threat to health but is more difficult to shed.*

As health is a primary concern, we can be grateful for the body wisdom that makes midriff fat easier to lose. But where appearance is involved, it can be difficult to deal with the body's choice to cling stubbornly to the fat stored in the upper legs and buttocks. Happily, exercise will help to reduce body fat stores all over the body. So will a low-fat eating plan. Thus, the IDEAL Weight-Loss Program can help you to trim your body fat stores *wherever they are located.*

BEING FAT IS NOT A SIN

It occurred to me about two years ago that eating had become the last bona fide sin left in America. . . . You see, sex was now "healthy" and "normal," while eating was "evil" and "perverted." The same people who read *The Joy of Sex* in public would only eat Reese's Peanut Butter Cups in the closet. The people who were happy after intercourse were guilty after the dessert course.

—Ellen Goodman, syndicated columnist*

Do you regard your eating habits as morally "bad," your excess fat stores as an all too visible sign that you are fundamentally "weak"? If you starve yourself and force yourself to exercise out of guilt, you won't do it for very long. Fat is not a moral issue, and neither is eating or not eating. Fat is a biological, physiological fact; eating and overeating have biological, physiological, and psychological determinants. Once you understand the scientific facts about fat, you will be able to stop acting as if food and eating have moral elements and a power over you that in reality do not exist. *You* have personal power. Fat is merely stored energy. Why make it any more significant than it really is?

FAT IS AN EVOLUTIONARY MIRACLE

Believe it or not, most of our ancestors were grateful for their fat stores. In times of famine, only the fattest survived. The human body had to adapt to an undependable feeding schedule by evolving "the starvation response." When food was unavailable, the bodies of our ancestors would slow down in response, thereby requiring less fuel in order to continue functioning. Then when food again became available, our forebears would overeat—partly out of physical and psychological hunger, but also due to the strong biological drive to replenish their depleted fat stores. At such times, their bodies would become exceptionally efficient at storing calories as fat to prepare for the next famine.

These days, in our well-fed society, famines are rare indeed. But our bodies still respond to periods of caloric inadequacy—nowadays self-induced—with the old starvation response. But when food becomes available again, the body's metabolism doesn't read the second signal. Your intake goes back up, but your resting metabolic rate stays down. Further, when we stop self-imposed restrictive dieting, we usually find ourselves overeating to make up for the deprivation. We may feel *compelled* to eat, *driven* to binge, *out of control* after going off yet another fad diet. The reason for such behavior is biological as well as psychological. You can blame it on your ancestors instead of harshly condemning yourself.

FAMILY TIES

And there are additional relatives on whom you can cast blame for your excess fat stores! Efficient fat storage can be an inherited trait, passed on from parents to children. (You may already blame your father and mother for many of your current woes, so why not add your weight problem to the list?) Perhaps of equal influence on future outcomes, family habits with food and exercise can be instilled at an early age and practiced for a lifetime. If you come from a family of constant nibblers and high-fat snackers with an aversion to exercise, it is easy to see how you developed your own eating and exercise habits.

SAY YES TO GIRTH CONTROL

If you have Low-Calorie Overweight, it is true that it's not your fault. But blaming your body, your ancestors, your family and loved ones will do little to help you *take control* of the situation. In order to make changes in your body weight, fat stores, level of fitness, and self-image, you will need to *take full responsibility for your body and your life*. You can make dramatic alterations in the way you look and feel. The choice is yours to make.

To determine whether you suffer from Diet-Induced, Low-Calorie Overweight, complete the following questionnaire. Record your answers in your IDEAL Log. I give you a point-scoring system for your answers right after the questionnaire. (If you are already quite certain that you have Low-Calorie Overweight, you may want to complete the questionnaire anyway, in order to expand your current level of personal insight and understanding.) You may want to make a photocopy of the questionnaire to insert with your answers in your log for future reference.

Self-Diagnosis of Low-Calorie Overweight

1. Weight History
- What is your present weight?
- How long have you been at this weight?
- When did you gain the extra poundage you now want to lose?
- Was there a single stress-related incident that preceded the weight gain (e.g., divorce, job change, pregnancy)? If so, describe briefly.
- Do you remember thinking that you gained too much weight during puberty?
- What was your maximum/highest weight as an adult?
- What has been your minimum weight as an adult?
- How much weight do you want to lose?

2. Family History
- Are/were either of your parents overweight?
- Are/were both of your parents overweight?
- Are/were any of your siblings overweight?
- Are/were any of your relatives morbidly obese (i.e., more than 100 pounds overweight)?
- Does/did anyone in your immediate family suffer from any of the following obesity-related medical conditions: diabetes, hypertension (high blood pressure), hyperlipidimia (elevated blood cholesterol)?
- Does your family exhibit an identifiable, perhaps cultural attitude toward body size/shape? If so, describe briefly.
- Does your diet reflect any identifiable ethnic preferences? If so, describe briefly.
- Did your family suffer from food shortages or other diet-related issues that may have affected your eating habits? If so, describe briefly.

3. Dieting History
- Have you ever attempted to lose weight on a fad diet (e.g., low-carbohydrate diet, rice diet, fruit-only diet)?
- Do you often try out the popular "quick weight-loss" diets as they appear?

- Have you ever tried to lose weight on a low-calorie diet (i.e., 1000 calories per day or less)?
- Do you often restrict your caloric intake (e.g., 1000 calories per day or less) for *short* periods?
- Is your *typical* caloric intake restricted (e.g., 1000 calories per day or less)?
- Do you find it impossible to lose weight, even when your caloric intake is restricted (e.g., 1000 calories per day or less)?
- Have you successfully lost weight in the past (e.g., ten to fifteen pounds in a few weeks), only to regain it a few months after the diet was abandoned?
- Do you weigh more now than you did before you started trying to diet?

4. Physical and Psychological History
- Do you often experience any of the following physical symptoms:

    Dry skin, dry hair
    Intolerance to cold, poor circulation
    Slow pulse
    Dizziness or lightheadedness (especially on standing or arising from bed)
    Fatigue, lethargy
    Tiredness after eight hours of sleep
    Constipation, bloating, cramps
    Poor sleep
    Poor memory
    Inability to concentrate and preoccupation with thoughts of food

- Do you often experience some or all of the following psychological symptoms:

    Distractibility and irritability
    Eating-related guilt and depression
    Constant compulsion to be on a diet and overwhelming guilt when not dieting
    Anger, frustration, feelings of victimization and outer-imposed (i.e., societal and cultural) control

Feelings of failure, weakness, susceptibility to temptations

Belief that your own self-concept and others' opinions of you are based mostly/entirely on what your body looks like

Belief that dietary restraint and eternal vigilance are required at all times in order to control your weight

Living in the future conditional (i.e., feel your life is on hold until *after* the diet)

Overall sense that food/diet dominates your life, that eating/not eating preoccupies your time and attention, that your body/overweight condition is responsible for the dissatisfaction in your life

5. Eating Behavior History

- Do you have an "either/or" attitude toward dieting (i.e., either you are "on a diet" or you are "pigging out" and the diet is "blown")?
- Do you eat more when you are sedentary? Do you eat less when you are physically active?
- Do you have difficulty determining when you are physically hungry? when you are satiated?
- Do you ignore physical hunger when you are dieting?
- Do you often starve yourself for a day, a few days, or longer?
- Do you sometimes embark on uncontrolled eating binges?
- Do you ever binge and purge (i.e., overeat, followed by self-induced vomiting or use of diuretics/laxatives)?
- Do you often skip breakfast? skimp on lunch? snack all evening?
- Do you use dietetic/low-calorie foods? "light" foods? diet drinks? artificial sweeteners?
- Do you often eat for reasons other than physical hunger (e.g., unconscious nibbling, nervous snacking, boredom-induced eating, holiday bingeing, pre- or post-diet bingeing)?
- Do you have many self-imposed dietary rules, "forbidden" foods that you try to avoid, special food rituals that you follow when dieting?
- Do you look at a diet as a short-term program?
- Do you regard each new diet as "the last diet" you will ever have to go on, the "final cure" for your weight problem?
- Could you be classified as a "chronic dieter"?

Your Self-Diagnosis

The key to diagnosing Low-Calorie Overweight can be found in section 3. *If you answered "yes" to the final three questions under Dieting History,* you undoubtedly have Low-Calorie Overweight. Give yourself 25 points.

Use the rest of your answers to the questionnaire to evaluate the extent of the problem. The more points you score, the more severe your genetic, diet-related, physical, psychological, and behavioral symptoms:

- *Weight history*—The pattern of weight gain over time indicates the onset and course of Low-Calorie Overweight. If your answers to this section reveal notable and frequent weight *fluctuations,* marked *deviations* from your desired weight, give yourself 1 point.
- *Family history*—Genetic and familial factors influence the development and course of Low-Calorie Overweight. If one of your parents was/is overweight, give yourself 1 point; if both parents were/are overweight, score 2 points; and add 1 point if you answered "yes" to more than three of the remaining six questions in section 2.
- *Dieting history*—The more low-calorie diets you've tried, the more severe the symptoms of your Low-Calorie Overweight condition may be. Score 3 points for each "yes" answer for the first five questions, plus 5 for each "yes" answer for the final three questions. (But if you answered "yes" to all three, remember to give yourself 25 points—*you have Low-Calorie Overweight.*)
- *Physical and psychological history*—The more physical and emotional side effects you are experiencing, the more severe your Low-Calorie Overweight symptoms. If you answered "yes" to more than five questions in section 4, give yourself 5 points.
- *Eating behavior history*—Your attitude toward eating and dieting can indicate the severity of your Low-Calorie Overweight symptoms. If you answered "yes" to more than one question, score 5 points.

Tally up your points to obtain your final score. *If you scored 25 points, you have Low-Calorie, Diet-Induced Overweight.* If your score exceeds 35 points, you may have a severe case. Fortunately, Diet-Induced Overweight—both mild and severe cases—*can* be treated with the IDEAL (I Don't Eat A Lot) program.

LOW-CALORIE OVERWEIGHT? OVEREATING? ℞: IDEAL

Now you know for sure whether or not your weight problem is due to Diet-Induced Overweight. If it is, the IDEAL Weight-Loss Program is the treatment of choice. And if you are fortunate enough not to suffer from this common disorder, you can still benefit from the program. This is the cure you've been seeking for your overweight problem. It entails taking *responsibility* for your condition and making the changes in your *lifestyle* required for living the fit, not fat, way.

There are four steps to making lifestyle change:

1. Self-evaluate—accurately and honestly.
2. Set goals—reasonably and realistically.
3. Personalize a plan—using the IDEAL Weight-Loss Program.
4. Put your plan into practice—*do it!*

On this program, you will find yourself evaluating and reevaluating your activity levels and eating habits, setting and resetting exercise, dietary, body weight, and fat goals. You will personalize an exercise plan that suits your individual goals and skills. You will personalize an eating plan that suits your individual goals and tastes. You will then put the program into practice—*you'll do it.* And you'll be eternally glad that you did!

WEIGHT WISE

Probably the first goal you have in mind—and may have been working toward off and on for some time now—is your desired weight. You desperately want to weigh 110 pounds, or 125 pounds, or 150 or 175. There is nothing inherently wrong with setting a personal weight goal, as long as you remember that *the numbers on the scale are not an accurate indication of how much body fat you have*. Your body consists of lean muscle tissue, bones, and bodily fluids, as well as fat. When you step on the scales, the number reflected there includes all these constituents. If you have just eaten, the weight of your food will be included in your scale weight. Food still in your digestive tract, dehydration or overhydration, monthly fluid retention, seasonal changes in humidity—all these and various other factors contribute to the number you see when you weigh yourself. How much body fat you may (or may not) need to lose is only one part of the equation.

Don't be a slave to the scales! Use your scale weight as *only one of your guidelines* for monitoring fat loss. (A number of more meaningful ways to measure success are provided in chapter 12.) When weight is lost in the form of fluids, the results are only temporary. This is exactly what happens with crash diets on which the body quickly eliminates water, making the numbers on the scale go down. You are seeking *permanent fat loss*, not fleeting fluid reductions and seductive but misleading weight decreases.

As one of your personal goals, determine a reasonable, realistic *healthy weight* for you to strive toward:

- Determine your current weight on a balance-beam scale, at home or in a health club or local medical facility. (Be sure to weigh yourself without clothing, first thing in the morning before breakfast. If you have a bathroom scale at home, you may want to calibrate it against a balance-beam scale.)
- Use your Body Mass Index results and "desirable" weight range from page 24 and, also taking your current weight and your weight history into account, select a healthy weight goal.
- If desired, set a comfortable weight goal *outside* of the given range. For example, if you weighed 135 in high school and felt great, even though 120 to 130 is the average for your body size, that may feel too low for you.
- Do not select an unreasonably low weight, as this will only lead to discouragement and unnecessary self-abuse.
- Record your current weight and healthy weight goal in your IDEAL Log.

Next, for a more useful assessment tool, use the Body Fat Percent chart that follows to help you select a healthy body fat goal. At a local sports medicine clinic, health club, or nutritionist's office, you can get your body fat percent measured with a simple assessment tool, calipers. Record your current and desired body fat percents in your IDEAL Log. Be sure to set a realistic body fat goal. You can always reset your goals once you meet them. Making slow, steady progress always feels a lot more rewarding than failure to attain impractical, arbitrary goals.

BODY FAT PERCENT RANGES

	% Body Fat for Males	% Body Fat for Females
Athletes	<10	<17
Lean	10–15	17–22
Normal	15–18	22–25
Above average	18–20	25–29
Overfat	20–25	29–35
Obese	25+	35+

IMMEDIATE GRATIFICATION

The very first day I jogged and walked for twenty minutes at my local high school track, *I felt better.* I hadn't lost any weight, my "love handles" were still intact, but I began to experience a sense of self-satisfaction. I was *doing something* to get in shape. I was becoming a different person inside. This provided me with an inner glow, a sort of spiritual lift that motivated me to keep going on my program, even when the going got tough.

I'm not going to tell you that the transformation was easy. But I will say this: I enjoyed the process. *You* deserve to feel good, too!

START SLOW, START SMALL, BUT START!

If you are still unsure about committing yourself to the program, remember that one of the main components of both the eating and exercise plans presented here is to *take it slowly*. In order to make permanent lifestyle changes, it is essential to *start small*. You can take careful, gradual, measured steps. On the road to fitness, your pace is unimportant. The important thing is to participate, to put your plan into practice, to do it! And you can take it *one step at a time*.

Actually, you've already taken the first step simply by beginning to read this book. And now, if you're ready, you can take another small step: Read the next chapter, and learn how to get yourself psyched up to begin on the IDEAL Weight-Loss Program.

3

*Getting Psyched for
Self-Change: Do It!*

*F*or many years, I ate four meals a day: breakfast, lunch, dinner, and midnight snack. Yes, the midnight snack was often a meal in itself. I would choose from ice cream, a piece of leftover pie, a good stack of cookies, a quarter-pound of cheese with crackers, a couple of brownies. Whatever I chose, I downed it all with a tall glass of whole milk or orange juice. The pattern had developed gradually after I became an adult, but actually I had seen it in action all of my life—my dad was a regular midnight snacker.

I knew this kind of eating wasn't doing me any good physically, but psychologically it felt good. I didn't know at the time that being a regular exerciser and a healthy eater, taking *control* of my life, would feel even better psychologically *and* do wonderful things for my body.

After I became a regular exerciser, I came to realize that if I hoped to progress further and feel even better, my eating habits had to change, too. *All* of my meals were too heavy on the fat. I would have to lower the fat in my diet. And if I were not to eliminate that fourth meal, I would surely have to change its content.

Finally, I admitted to myself that eating as I had been only felt good at the time; in fact, it was destructive in the long run. As I started to lower the fat in my diet significantly, my body's reaction to fatty foods changed, too. Now, if I happen to eat too much fat at any one time, my body feels bad right away and lets me know that I made a mistake.

THE FOUR STEPS

To change my harmful eating habits, I followed the four steps to implementing lifestyle change, the same steps I took to start on an exercise program:

1. I self-evaluated—accurately and honestly.
2. I set goals—flexibly and realistically.
3. I personalized my plan to suit my individual needs and life-style patterns.
4. I put the plan into practice—I *did it!*

I started by substituting low-fat foods for my evening munching, and slowly reduced the amounts I ate by shifting the bulk of my food intake to the daytime hours. Now I eat a solid breakfast, a light lunch, and a balanced dinner. I still have a fourth meal, but it's light—fresh or dried fruit, a few crackers, a modest glass of juice. I now go to bed satisfied instead of stuffed, and I wake up energetic and refreshed, with my appetite piqued for the day ahead. My diet is in balance, and I *feel* so much better!

I'm not saying it was easy to change my ways. And I won't lie to you and claim that I *never* indulge in a heavy late-night snack. I have setbacks every now and then, but I have learned to forgive myself and just go on. It's the overall healthy *balance* in my life that counts. Wrapping myself in a heavy cloak of guilt is not only useless, it's counterproductive. If I notice that I'm slipping back into my old nighttime patterns, I pull out my IDEAL Log and record my insights and feelings. This way, I can pinpoint what is causing the behavior, and then I can *take control* of it. This process works for me, and it can work for you, too.

EXAMINE YOUR ATTITUDE: DIG DEEP

"But I'm not a night eater," you say. "That's not *my* problem. I starve myself day *and* night, and I still can't lose weight!" You might want to take a close look at your eating patterns to see exactly how—and why—you eat. This means you have to dig down deep inside and evaluate your feelings. Remember, as the U.S. Surgeon General has said recently, healthy eating is much more a matter of controlling how much *fat* you eat than it is controlling how *much* you eat.

I've developed a comprehensive questionnaire to guide you. Be honest with yourself, but don't be too hard on yourself. We're all human, we all screw up now and again. Try to have a sense of humor about the whole thing. Recognizing that an "accidental" fat binge does not mark the end of the world is a lot easier on your psyche than hours of self-inflicted and counterproductive browbeating.

Use your personal diary, your trusty IDEAL Log, to record the answers to the Self-Evaluation: Fat Attitude. Complete this questionnaire in a single sitting, if possible, so that your train of introspective thought is uninterrupted. Choose a time and a setting where you can be alone for a while and able to concentrate deeply. It is a tough step to take, but it will lead you down the path to total fitness and a low-fat body.

Self-Evaluation: Fat Attitude

Part I: Your Food Fat Attitude

1. Which of these foodstuffs are bad for you?

Ice cream	Bran muffins	Red meat
Fast foods	Carrot cake	Eggs
White bread	Chocolate	Diet soft drinks

2. Which of these foodstuffs are good for you?

Tuna	Raw vegetables	Peanut butter
Cottage cheese	Fresh fruit	Liver
Yogurt	Popcorn, unbuttered	Diet soft drinks

3. Myth or fact? We should eat solely to satisfy physical needs, and not in response to psychological urges.
4. Myth or fact? A healthy diet excludes sweets and chocolate.
5. Myth or fact? It is best to eliminate from your diet those foods that tempt you to overeat.

Take a quick look through your kitchen before answering questions 6 through 10.

6. Is your refrigerator virtually empty, except perhaps for condiments and diet soft drinks? Describe the contents briefly.
7. Are your pantry shelves virtually empty, except perhaps for flour and other baking needs? Describe the contents briefly.
8. Is your freezer full of tempting foods such as super-premium ice cream, thick steaks, and bacon? Describe the contents briefly.
9. Are your kitchen cupboards stocked with tempting snack foods such as corn chips, commercial sandwich cookies, and Poptarts? Describe the contents briefly.
10. Does your kitchen illustrate how you are either depriving yourself or indulging yourself (i.e., there is either a paucity or an overabundance of foods)?
11. Can you recognize the physical signs of hunger? If so, describe them.
12. Do you ever ignore physical hunger?
13. Do you tend to skip breakfast? Do you tend to eat a light (or no) lunch? Do you eat your largest meal at night?
14. Do you embark on uncontrolled eating binges? If so, how often does this occur?
15. Do you ever eat for emotional reasons—that is, when you are feeling anxious or stressed, when you are angry, when you are depressed, when you are feeling lonely?
16. Do you ever find yourself eating without thinking—that is, nibbling while you're preparing meals, while cleaning up after meals, while watching television, while reading or working or talking on the telephone?
17. Do you ever overeat to the point of feeling stuffed? If so, does this usually occur during (or soon after) attempting to diet?
18. Have you ever starved yourself for a day? For longer than a

day? If so, describe how *long* and how *often* you have starved yourself.

19. Do you consider yourself to be a gourmet cook, a gourmet diner, or gourmand?
20. Do you exercise regularly? If so, do you tend to eat more after a workout than you do on non-workout days?

Part II: Your Body Fat Attitude

1. In your IDEAL Log, list all of the benefits of importance to *you* associated with losing weight (e.g., improved appearance, better social life, reduction in elevated blood pressure). Then list any drawbacks of personal concern (e.g., stress associated with becoming more attractive, loss of certain friends, fear of change). Be honest, use your insight, dig in!
2. List the reasons why you want to lose excess weight and become physically fit. Some common reasons are listed below.

INNER MOTIVATION	OUTER MOTIVATION
To feel better about myself	To look better to others
To like my body	To attract/please the opposite sex
To have more energy	
To improve my health	To join the fitness craze
To prevent ill health	To please my physician
To feel more self-confident	To please my family, friends
To feel proud of myself	To attract compliments
To feel successful, in control	To wear new, trendy styles of clothes

3. In your log, list the commitments from the selection that follows which you are now ready, willing, able to make:

   - To moderation in eating habits
   - To regularity in exercise
   - To patience and perseverance
   - To honesty in examining diet, exercise, lifestyle
   - To replacing old, unhealthy habits
   - To practicing new, healthful habits
   - To making gradual changes
   - To making permanent changes

4. Are you motivated to lose weight right now? Does your current attitude toward your body and your lifestyle indicate that you need and want to make changes? So, *are you going to undertake this program?* Record your answers.

Reviewing Your Self-Evaluation

Part I:

1–2.   These questions can reveal dichotomous diet-related thinking, that is, the attitude that low-calorie foods are "good" while sweets, snack foods, and high-calorie items are "bad." On the IDEAL Weight-Loss Program, there are few forbidden foods. The key is eating in moderation, not restrictive dieting.

3–5.   These are common diet-related myths that can lead to unhealthy eating practices, including self-deprivation and bingeing. The key to developing permanent, healthy eating habits is to learn to employ *moderation* and *control*. On the program, you will learn how to identify physical hunger and how to *satisfy your needs while you lose weight.* You will also learn to identify psychological cues to eat and how to appease food cravings without overdoing it.

6–10.   These questions can indicate an attitude of self-deprivation or self-indulgence, both of which can lead to eating binges.

11–12. These questions can help you to discover whether you are aware of the physical signs of hunger, as distinguished from environmental or emotional cues for eating.

13.   If you answered "yes" to these questions, you are a NIGHT EATER (as I used to be). This unhealthy, unbalanced eating pattern also induces weight *gain*. The program will help you to eliminate this pattern in favor of a healthful eating plan that induces weight *loss*.

14.   If you answered "yes" to this question and you indulge in the behavior on a frequent basis (e.g., once a month or more), you are a BINGE EATER. Binge eating is a com-

mon problem for chronic dieters and those with Low-Calorie Overweight, a disordered eating pattern that the program will help to eradicate.

15. If you answered "yes" to at least one of these questions, you are a STRESS EATER. The program will help you to identify the emotions that trigger undesirable eating responses; you will learn to respond in more appropriate, healthful ways.

16. If you answered "yes" to one or more of these questions, you are a MINDLESS NIBBLER. The program can show you how to pay attention to your eating habits in order to become a smart snacker and a more mindful diner.

17. If you answered "yes" to the first question, you are a STUFFER. Your overeating patterns have undoubtedly contributed to your overweight problem. If you answered "yes" to the second question, you are a STARVER-AND-STUFFER. The self-deprivation of low-calorie dieting is contributing to your weight problem by triggering a physiological and psychological drive to replenish yourself by overeating. You need to take control of your eating patterns. You need to adopt the program.

18. If you have starved yourself for a day or more, and do so on a regular basis, you are a STARVER. As you now know, a restricted caloric intake causes Low-Calorie Overweight. The program will teach you how to properly nourish yourself so you can stop starving and start losing weight.

19. Sometimes food connoisseurs overeat, either by *mindless nibbling* or with chronic *stuffing*. By diverting your attention to your food habits and the nutrient/fat contents of your dietary intakes, the IDEAL Weight-Loss Program allows for gourmet dining without overeating.

20. If you habitually overeat after exercising, you are a WORKOUT–PIG-OUT EATER. Regular exercise will actually assist you with appetite control, once you adopt the program and learn how to satisfy your physical and psychological postactivity dietary needs in a healthful manner.

Part II:

1–3.   Your lists can help you see whether you are ready, motivated, and willing to lose weight:

- If your list of benefits is longer than your list of drawbacks, you are now *ready* to lose that excess weight.
- If your list of reasons for losing weight includes more than three of the motivators given, you are indeed *motivated* to lose weight; if you included at least one of the indicated inner motivations, part of your drive to become fit comes from within—and is apt to last longer than any of the outer motivators that may be influencing you.
- If you included three or more of the commitments to weight loss in your own list, you are *willing* to make the effort required to change your lifestyle patterns in order to lose fat and get fit.

4.   If you answered "yes" to the final query in this question, then you are indeed ready, willing, and *able*. So, go ahead and *do it!*

WHAT MOTIVATES *YOU?*

The preceding self-evaluation should help you to uncover deep-seated attitudes about food, fat, and your body. In conducting my own soul search, I found that I actually was afraid to make certain lifestyle changes. I was fearful of failure, worried that I could never become an athlete and would never be able to give up my nightly snacking habit. But I also discovered that I was *motivated* to take a risk, that I felt the benefits of looking better and feeling fit were worth the effort required. I realized that I was *ready* to make a commitment to improving my dietary and exercise habits, that I wanted to become fit so much that I was also *willing* and (hopefully) *able* to make the necessary changes.

To successfully adopt and permanently adhere to the IDEAL program, it is essential for you to be motivated—and for the right reasons. *Outer motivation,* doing it for someone or something else, almost always dwindles away over time. That's because it isn't really yours, unlike the *inner motivation* that comes from within, from your heart and your soul. Take another look at the weight-control and fitness motivators in the self-evaluation on fat attitudes. If you can see that you really want to make lifestyle changes for yourself and for your own well-being, then you already have the necessary inner motivation. You're psyched up to begin to change. And if you can maintain inner motivation, you will be successful—I can guarantee it. If not, you may get all of your weight back—and more!

This chapter will provide you with a host of tips for maintaining inner motivation. I suggest you read through the entire chapter, then go back and reread the sections that seem to be addressing you. It may prove helpful to photocopy the tip sheets that cover your own personal issues and keep them in your IDEAL Log or post them in your kitchen, for easy access and ready reference whenever you need an inner motivation jump-start.

RECOGNIZING HUNGER

Did your self-evaluation reveal that you often eat when you are not physically hungry? This is certainly the case for those of us who are night eaters. After not eating (much) all day, I would indeed be hungry for dinner. My stomach would growl, reminding me to fill 'er up. But after a nice big dinner, I would continue to eat though I no longer was physically hungry. I was eating because I was bored or lonely or anxious about the days ahead. How about you:

- Do you eat just because the food is there?
- Do you habitually eat in front of the television?
- Do you stuff yourself at parties, overindulge on holidays, splurge in restaurants?
- Do you automatically eat lunch when the clock strikes noon, even if you are not physically hungry?
- Does a good workout make you want to go pig out?
- And do your strict diets inevitably lead to uncontrolled eating binges?

These are examples of environmentally induced eating behaviors, triggered not by true hunger but cued by the world around you. The list below illustrates typical *environmental eating cues*. You can take control of all such situations by recognizing the fact that it is you, not the environment around you, who is in charge.

Environmental Eating Cues

- Sight and smell of food
- Television viewing
- Media advertisements for food
- Supermarket shopping while hungry or dieting
- Cooking and clean-up while hungry or dieting
- Alcohol intake, parties, socializing around food
- Holiday celebrations and feasts
- Restaurant temptations
- Your spouse, children, parent(s), friend(s)
- The clock—noontime, dinner time, snack time, coffee break time
- The kitchen
- Leftovers
- Dieting

Sometimes we turn to food when emotions are charged, unconsciously (or consciously) avoiding our inner feelings. How about you:

- Do you often turn to the refrigerator when you feel bored or depressed?
- If you are upset or anxious, does an eating binge *temporarily* calm you?
- Is food one of your favorite "friends" to whom you turn when feeling lonely?
- Do you ever avoid doing unpleasant tasks and facing personal issues by eating instead?
- Do you sometimes stuff your face for the "energy" you need to face the day, or because you are mad as heck and need to gnaw on something?

- Do you reward yourself with food after a difficult day or after a day or two of self-starvation?
- *Do you let food have control over you?*

You can control all such emotional eating cues. Once you recognize the fact that it is you, not the food, who is in charge, you can learn to experience your emotions *without turning to food*. Exercise can help you in dealing with upsetting emotions. Overeating only serves to put off necessary self-confrontation—and makes the process of dealing with your feelings even more painful by adding in feelings of guilt.

Take a look at the list that follows, the most common emotional triggers for overeating. What can you do to *take control* of such emotions, instead of denying them and eating—when food is not what you really need?

Emotional Eating Cues

• Boredom	• Anger
• Depression	• Fatigue
• Deprivation	• Worry
• Stress	• Procrastination
• Loneliness	• Self-reward
• Holiday tension	• Feeling out of control
• Celebration anxiety	

The first step is to learn to differentiate between true physical hunger and the urge to eat for nonphysical reasons. True hunger is indicated by a hollow, empty feeling in the gut, usually accompanied by stomach rumblings. This physical drive to refuel occurs four to six hours after a meal and will be present upon arising in the morning (unless you are a night eater).

Once you identify *why* you want to eat—that is, for physical or emotional reasons—then you can decide whether or not you *will* eat. Because the choice is yours. You are not a victim of the world around you, and you are not under a magic spell cast by the food that is all too available to us. *You are the master of your destiny,* not the victim of fate. So, the next time you feel the urge to eat, *stop and think:*

- Are you really physically hungry?
- If not, what is it you are really feeling? Are you nervous, bored, depressed, or angry for some reason?
- Will eating do anything to help how you are feeling? How?
- Would dealing with the environment and your emotions *without eating* prove to be a more productive step for you to take? Could a brisk walk calm your tension? It would certainly give you something productive to do. Might a humorous movie lift your mood? Perhaps you need to confront someone honestly and bravely, instead of burying yourself in your well-stocked kitchen?

Practice getting in touch with your feelings and acting on them. If you feel vaguely or highly unsettled, take the time to figure out exactly what it is you are feeling. Are you lonely? Call up a friend. Are you drained of energy, physically and mentally fatigued? Take a nap. Food is not the appropriate antidote to disturbing emotional stirrings. Identifying and dealing with your emotions is the healthy way to heal your inner wounds.

With patience and practice, eventually you will begin to find that it is second nature for you to tap into your innermost self. This is not an easy process for most of us. It is a lot easier simply to grab those chocolate chip cookies and stuff them down—along with the feelings that triggered the urge to eat. But once you begin to practice getting in touch with yourself, you will see how much better that feels than burying or camouflaging your *real* needs and personal problems with sweets and snack foods. And the end result is that you will take control of your eating and your life. There are few better feelings than the self-empowerment that comes from being in charge of your life.

NIGHT EATING

I found a number of common-sense behavioral adjustments made it possible for me to give up night eating binges without excessive emotional stress. Even if night eating is not a problem for you, the tips that follow might prove useful. Everyone can benefit from drinking adequate fluids, for example, especially when exercising regularly, as we do on this program. And eating regular meals, including a hearty breakfast, is a wise habit for all of us to adopt.

Note that adherence to the program should help you curb the overall urge to binge eat. The starvation response of low-calorie dieting triggers a compelling physiological drive to overeat following the prolonged self-starvation. By consuming adequate amounts of nutritious food in well-balanced daily meals, the physical and psychological pressure to binge—at night or anytime—will disappear.

A Baker's Dozen Tips for Night Eaters

1. Set a deadline time after which you do not eat (e.g., no food after seven P.M.).
2. Drink plenty of water all day and throughout the evening to quench thirst and feel a sense of fullness.
3. Reduce television watching, especially late at night, or substitute noneating behaviors for snacking during television viewing (e.g., riding a stationary bike or knitting).
4. Exercise in the evening to reduce appetite.
5. Go for a brisk walk after dinner.
6. Join a health club and work out in the evenings; on nonworkout nights, enjoy a sauna or a massage.
7. Get out of the kitchen—or out of the house—after dinner.
8. Do your food shopping *after* a meal, when everything edible does not seem so tempting.
9. Make a well-balanced breakfast a morning ritual.
10. Avoid skimpy lunches in favor of a well-balanced noontime meal.
11. Avoid meal skipping, self-starvation, and low-calorie dieting, which will inevitably trigger binge eating at vulnerable times (like bedtime).
12. If eating in the evening seems to trigger binges, limit all snacks to daytime hours.
13. Establish a regular routine with meal eating and daily exercise, then practice it until it feels natural. (Be patient with yourself; old habits die hard!)

EUSTRESS VS. DISTRESS

Do you eat when you feel stressed? Do you often overeat when you are tense, anxious, uptight? And does eating or overeating ever really *solve the problem?*

Life can be stressful, especially in our demanding society. But stress isn't all bad. In fact, it can serve as a productive source of stimulation. It is *how you deal with stress* that makes the difference between feeling overwhelmed and being in control. If you try to ignore stress or let stressful situations drive you to drink or eat, this is *distress,* which is unhealthful and counterproductive. But if you face up to stress and learn how to manage and control stressful situations, you will find that stress can be healthy for you, challenging and with productive end results. The stress which provides you with the opportunity to grow and change is known as *eustress,* or beneficial stress.

Exercise stresses the body. This is healthful stress, building muscle tissue and strengthening bones, improving cardiovascular function, and enhancing physical endurance.

Remember that it is your attitude toward stressful situations that determines whether you feel out of control and under duress or in charge and stimulated by the challenges that face you. The choice is yours!

The tips below can help you to better manage everyday stress. And on the program, you will automatically reduce the stress associated with chronic dieting, as well as control distress through regular exercise. Thus, you'll be on your way to living a healthier life—in spite of the unavoidable stresses of today's world.

A Dozen Tips to Reduce Stress

1. Exercise is the natural antidote to stress, so make regular physical activity a daily habit.
2. Meditation can decrease blood lactate and increase alpha brain wave activity, providing a natural "up" and inducing feelings of relaxation.
3. Escape the tyranny of the bathroom scales by measuring success in more meaningful ways (see chapter 12).

4. Replace the search for perfectionism with realistic goals, then congratulate yourself (often) for successfully attaining them.

5. Don't put off making changes. Procrastination of desired changes can provoke more anxiety than actually *making* the changes, and it always prolongs the agony.

6. If your lifestyle causes constant stress, try to adjust your pace and reduce your activities to a more manageable level, so that you can feel healthy as well as productive.

7. Practice being introspective and getting in touch with your feelings so that you will be able to identify the sources of your stress.

8. Whenever you feel guilty, reassess the situation to determine why, and then substitute a less stress-inducing attitude.

9. Trade in black-and-white, all-or-nothing thinking for an attitude favoring moderation in all things.

10. Have a sense of humor about life. Laughter can be a great way to relieve tension.

11. Accept the inevitability of change and regard life's stresses as challenges instead of as sources of suffering.

12. Take control of your life. This is the most important factor in managing stress, staying healthy, and being emotionally and physically fit.

MORAL (NOT ORAL) SUPPORT

Are you afraid to ask for help when you need it? Does everyone rely on *you* for support, but you have only your favorite brand of super-premium ice cream to turn to in times of need? An important aspect of being in control of your life is knowing when to ask for outside aid and knowing how to nourish yourself—without food. The key is to realize that *you deserve support and nourishment*. Once you admit that you are worthy of others' attention and your own self-care, then you will be able to seek—and secure—what you need.

We often turn to food in situations when far more appropriate forms of fulfillment could be selected. It is certainly easier to eat whenever you feel needy, but does this ever solve the real problem? When you are in need of a caring hug, will a bag of potato chips really do the trick? When you are in need of intellectual stimulation or physical exertion, will a box of Oreos serve the same purpose? Why deny yourself the nonedible emotional nurturing you crave? Remember, you are changing your old lifestyle patterns because you know that you are worth the effort. You have decided to exercise regularly and eat well because you have realized *you deserve to feel good*. And you are going to shed your excess poundage in order to attain and maintain a healthy, attractive physique because you understand that *you deserve to feel good about yourself.* So, don't deprive yourself of the support you know that you merit. Seek it from nonfood sources, and feel good about helping yourself to feel good. You deserve it!

The tips below help me to select inedible sources of nurturing whenever I feel the need. You may want to utilize my list or create your own. You know exactly what—and who—can make you feel really good about yourself. And feeling great is, after all, what this program is all about.

A Dozen Tips for Nonedible Nourishment

1. Go to a film after dinner instead of heading for the ice cream parlor.
2. Buy a new pair of walking shoes with the money you save from spending less on food.
3. Invest in a ten-speed bicycle or purchase a stationary bicycle, a free weight set, and a stationary rowing machine, and set up your own home gym.
4. Join a health club and enjoy the fringe benefits—sauna, jacuzzi, masseuse, etc.—as well as your regular workouts there.
5. After a good workout, reward yourself with a long hot bath in place of too much food and drink.
6. Enroll in a class to learn meditation, the martial arts, or other forms of controlled relaxation.
7. Call up or visit with a sympathetic friend when you need moral support.
8. Ask for support from family and friends, not as a sign of

weakness, but as an honest commitment to making significant lifestyle changes.

9. Ask for votes of confidence and occasional praise for your
new self, not as outer motivation, but for the nourishment of
a subtle morale boost that can come from someone who
cares.

10. Practice writing down your feelings in your IDEAL Log
instead of stuffing them down inside with food.

11. Accept the responsibility for determining exactly what you
are "hungry" for—attention, love, friendship, fun, excitement, change—and then, go get it!

12. Instead of waiting impatiently for the end result, *enjoy the
process* for what it is: getting fitter, taking control of your
life, and living in balance.

FEAR OF FAILURE—OR SUCCESS?

When I first thought about beginning an exercise program, I
didn't trust myself enough to explore my limits, nor did I respect
myself enough to accept my limitations. When I finally decided
that I wanted, needed, had to become active, I was determined to
succeed. So I did. I had set sensible, reasonable goals. I decided to
explore my limits: How far could I go? But I recognized my
limitations, whatever they might be. I wouldn't be achieving goals
overnight. However, I knew I would make major changes over the
long run, and I continue to meet new goals every year. Succeeding
is a terrific feeling.

When I decided to alter my eating habits, I once again had to
face my inner fears. Would I go crazy without a cookie fix?
Wouldn't all the PaceWalking, running, biking, and swimming
invoke an appetite I couldn't control? This type of fearful thought
clouded my head until I finally *just did it*. As soon as I made a true
commitment to eating well, the fears went away.

Change is an inevitable process of life. Only one thing in life
never changes, and that is the fact that everything is always
changing. The key to success is to take control of change, to *make
changes yourself* rather than feel that changes just happen to you.
If you decide that you want to change your lifestyle, that you want

to exercise regularly and eat healthfully, that you want to lose that extra weight and keep it off, you *can* succeed. By taking control of your lifestyle and your body, *you* choose and *you* make the desired changes.

UNLOCKING INNER PRISONS

Now that I've allowed myself to be the athlete I never thought I could be, I feel like I've been let out of an inner prison. Unless you realize that you are in an inner prison, you can't let yourself out. Ask yourself the following questions to see whether you are trapped in the prison of your own mind:

- Do you stop yourself from trying new and unfamiliar activities because you doubt your abilities?
- Do you harshly restrict your food intake because you don't trust yourself with food?
- Do you serve yourself a meager bread-and-water diet of self-disrespect, treating yourself like a dangerous criminal instead of a trusted friend?
- Have you put your life on hold, not allowing yourself to enjoy your day-to-day living, or to even like yourself, until after the "sentence" (i.e., latest diet) is over?

I have some liberating words of advice for you: Give yourself a break, and commute your self-imposed sentence. From now on, whenever you find yourself locked in your inner prison, let yourself out. Whenever you put yourself down, doubt yourself, or blast yourself, try substituting a more lenient sentence. Replace unproductive, failure-inducing negative thoughts with the morale-boosting positive self-image that you deserve.

Whenever you find yourself thinking negatively or putting yourself down, tell your mind to STOP. Then, from the list below, select the appropriate counterthought and repeat the indicated self-supportive statement to yourself several times. Eventually, positive thinking will become second nature to you, as habitual and as natural as your negative thoughts may be right now.

COUNTERTHOUGHT SELF-SUPPORT TO OFFSET SELF-DEPRECATION

Typical Self-Deprecatory Thought: STOP!	Substitute Self-Supportive Counterthought: REPEAT
I'm always a failure on diets.	Diets have failed me in the past, but this time *I'm* in charge.
I have no willpower.	I choose to use my personal power to elicit my desired lifestyle changes.
Eating well/exercising regularly is too hard.	Eating well/exercising regularly is a *challenge.*
I'm out of control around food.	I have personal power; food does not control me.
I have no control over the things that happen to me.	I am the master of my destiny, not a victim of fate.
There is no way I can avoid "blowing" it today.	I will be moderate because *I* am in control.
I already blew it—it's all over now.	Setbacks are inevitable, so it's no big deal.
My body will never look thin enough.	Health and fitness are my goals, and in attaining them I *will* shed excess body fat.
I'll never look like a movie star or a fashion model.	I accept myself as I am, and I'm working on improving my physical self to meet my own personal potential.
I want my body, diet, and lifestyle to be perfect.	*Nobody's* perfect, but I'm improving.

Typical Self-Deprecatory Thought: STOP!	Substitute Self-Supportive Counter-thought: REPEAT
I will never eat _____ again. *(Fill in the blank.)*	I will eat _____ in moderation if I so choose, because *I* am in control.
I will never miss a day of exercise again.	Exercise makes me feel good, but I'll rest when my body needs to.
I'm fat; I'm a bad person.	Fat is *not* a moral issue; I'm a good person.
My body is ugly.	I like myself, and my body will soon show this.
I'm too clumsy to be athletic.	I'm trying hard, and I'm getting better at it.
I'm too fat to exercise in public.	Exercise makes me feel good, and I deserve to feel good.
Other people are so much thinner, fitter, more attractive, better than I am.	I'm working on improving myself, and that's all that matters.
I *should* lose weight, I know I *should*.	I will lose weight because *I* want to, for *me*.
Why do I have to be fat? Why me?	I am the master of my destiny, not a victim of fate.
My life would be totally different if I weren't fat.	I accept my life as it is, and I will be responsible for it.
I'm afraid that I'll fail—again.	This time I'm ready to succeed.
I'm afraid of what will happen if I succeed.	I'm excited about my new life ahead.
I'm never going to be thin, fit, in shape.	I am getting leaner and more fit day by day.

Typical Self-Deprecatory Thought: STOP!	Substitute Self-Supportive Counterthought: REPEAT
This is taking too long—nothing is happening.	I am making slow, steady progress.
Starving makes me feel moral, heroic.	I deserve to eat well.
No one understands my feelings.	I can share my feelings and benefit from others' support.
I can't deal with stress.	Stress is inevitable, so I'll use it to my advantage.
I'm not a healthy person.	I am healthy because I want to be healthy.
I can't do it.	I *can* do it, I *will* do it, I *am* doing it!
I'll never change.	I'm capable of continuous change.
I'll always be fat.	I'm in control and *I* choose to be fit, not fat.

ACCEPTING YOUR UNIQUE PHYSIQUE

When I finally accepted the fact that I would never have a build like Rocky, it was liberating to face the reality that I would not have a perfect body in this lifetime! I have now accepted the one I was genetically programmed to be in, and I am working hard on improving it to achieve the greatest potential possible. I'm happy with what I have and willing to make the best of it—as you should be. Why not select reasonable goals that you can indeed achieve?

Do you have a realistic self-image? Perhaps you are picturing yourself as a fatter person than you really are! The societal pressure to conform to overly thin model images may have contributed to a distorted self-image. A skewed body image, formed from years of comparing yourself to unrealistic ideals and then disliking yourself, could be adding to your self-dissatisfaction.

I have devised a self-evaluation that you can do to see whether your body image is distorted. Perhaps you will discover that you are not nearly as fat as you think. This should help you to feel better about the body you have now, the one you are trying to improve—gradually, permanently. And even if this is not true for you, try accepting yourself *the way you are right now.* The accompanying Body Image Activity can help you to do so by enabling you to compare your *self*-image with your *mirror* image in order to unskew any *false* images you may have.

BODY IMAGE ACTIVITY

You will need three sheets of plain white paper (8½ × 11"), a sharp pencil, and a full-length mirror. Use your IDEAL Log to record the results, your comments, and your feelings. Select a time when you can conduct this fifteen-minute activity undisturbed.

1. Without looking in the mirror, sketch an outline of your current body shape *as you picture it* in your own mind. Try to draw a figure that illustrates proportion sizes for target areas: How big is your waist compared to your hips? What do your thighs look like compared to the remainder of your legs? And your upper arms, how are they shaped? Be as accurate as you can, and be honest. After all, you will never have to display your self-portrait publicly.
2. On a second sheet of paper, sketch an outline of the body shape you consider to be *ideal for you.* Be realistic, and be reasonable. Draw your potential body shape, the physique you are actually going to be able to attain and maintain on the IDEAL Weight-Loss Program.
3. Stand in front of the mirror and objectively appraise your body shape. Sketch your figure *as you see it* on the third sheet of paper. Try to replicate the actual proportions of your current physique, especially the relative sizes for the target areas (i.e., waist, hips, thighs—wherever you need reshap-

ing). Again, try to draw your figure as accurately as you are able. Try not to exaggerate your flaws, but don't overlook them either.

4. Compare your three drawings and ask yourself the following questions:

- Do you imagine your body the way it actually appears? Or do you picture yourself as fatter—or thinner—than you really are?
- Is your ideal body shape far different from your actual figure? Or is your body shape goal a thinned-down version of your current self?
- Are you too hard on yourself—that is, do you exaggerate your flaws and/or aim for perfection? Could you tone down your expectations somewhat and still attain self-satisfaction?

Save your sketches for future reference. You may want to reexamine the ideal body shape drawing once you have achieved your IDEAL weight-loss goals. It is always inspirational to have available some *before* and *after* "pictures" of yourself.

A SOCIETY FIT FROM WITHIN

The so-called New Age we are living in is a time of rapid personal and social change. With the dawning of this new era comes the revelation that we have control as individuals, that we can make changes—starting with ourselves. For many, the New Age is a metaphor for the changes occurring in various aspects of our daily lives. For some, New Age pursuits mean the fringe interests of crystals and channeling. But for most, it represents the practical matter of creating a society that lives in harmony with itself, with nature, with the cosmos. Living in the New Age entails developing a new view of life from a different perspective. And the work must begin with ourselves, as we change from the inside out, moving toward social transformation via reenergizing personal development.

The chance to begin to change our world lies within each of us. We can start by changing ourselves, by harmonizing our inner and outer beings, by growing healthier, getting fit, taking control of our bodies and our lives. Inner development, spiritual balance, can be a source of *your* inner motivation, as it is for me. And it will be your inner motivation that will propel your progress, both on the program and on your life's path.

So take the first step toward changing yourself—for your inner and outer self, for good. Start by going for a walk! The next section will give you all of the information you need to make PaceWalking an enjoyable part of your new, healthy, well-balanced lifestyle.

The Exercise Plan That Lets You Eat More

4

PaceWalking: The Ideal Exercise to Start—Now!

*L*ate one night in September 1985, I was slowly completing my first Ironman distance triathlon. I had about ten miles to go. It was dark, cold, and lonely, but I was on my way to the finish line. I had just switched from running slowly to walking briskly for the last time. I was going to make it.

I had swum the required 2.4 miles in open saltwater, ridden the 112 miles of rolling Cape Cod terrain on my bike, and was now coming in on the return leg of the 26.2-mile (marathon) run leg. My goal had been simply to finish the race under the seventeen-hour time limit. And I wanted to be both happy and healthy when I crossed the finish line.

Well, I beat the time limit, happily and healthily. It took me sixteen hours and forty-two minutes, precisely twice the time that the winner, Scott Tinley, had taken in setting the then world's record for the distance. We each had a great day (well, for him, day; for me, day *and* night). So how did I, a former nonathlete but recent four-times-a-week jogger, do this?

Well, before the race, I had figured out that I could reasonably maintain a pace in each of the three legs that would allow me to beat the deadline: forty-minute miles in the swim, fourteen miles per hour on the bike, and fourteen-minute miles in the marathon. I also figured out that, based on my previous marathon experience, I would be much better off if I alternated running and fast walking in that segment. And that's what I did. In the course of doing so, I discovered PaceWalking. I even started thinking about writing a book about it—during the race!

By alternating walking and running, I was able to conserve my dwindling energy supplies and minimize the pounding on my tired muscles. During the final ten-mile stretch, I realized that I would actually do better if I briskly walked the rest of the way. I was right. It worked. I felt terrific. And I had discovered for myself a new form of exercise that I really enjoyed. It's a sport that almost anyone can do. There's no need for you to enter an Ironman triathlon to enjoy the mental and physical benefits of PaceWalking.

There are now an estimated 5 million serious walkers striding about the United States. For those over age forty-five, walking has really come into vogue, attracting former (injured) joggers and nonexercisers in droves. As Dr. Paul Dudley White, the late world-renowned cardiologist, once explained, "Walking is the easiest exercise for most individuals, one that can be done without equipment except good shoes, in almost any terrain and weather, and into very old age."

Of course, walking is not new. Thomas Jefferson advised early Americans, "Walking is the best exercise of all." What *is* new is the scientific evidence showing that fast walking is as beneficial an aerobic exercise as running, cycling, or aerobic dance. The choice of walking for a habitual exercise routine—to get in shape, to lose fat and build muscle—is a relatively recent phenomenon. Walking was once regarded as too simple, too accessible, too painless to be taken seriously. It was too hard to believe that the *best* exercise was actually the *easiest*. In fact, walking used to be reserved for the cooling down period *after* the completion of other aerobic exercises, such as jogging or biking.

Aerobic (a Greek word meaning air and life) exercise is any rhythmic, repetitive physical activity that involves one or more major muscle groups, such as the legs, and leads to an increase in their use of oxygen. Aerobic exercise speeds up the heart, but to a healthy degree. It strengthens the cardiovascular system, as well as building up muscle size and strength. With aerobic exercise, you need not huff and puff nor "go for the burn." Aerobic dancing, for example, has been refined to "soften" the activity in order to prevent injury and burn-out. Pain is *not* necessarily gain. Enjoyment and endurance, feeling fit and feeling good *are*.

PaceWalking is not racewalking, the sport in which participants speed along at a tricky, hip-swinging gait while making pronounced arm movements. Racewalkers have learned an exhilarating but technically difficult sport, one that has been largely ignored by the American public. But it is aerobic walking, what I call PaceWalking, *not* racewalking, that has become part of the fitness explosion.

Walking, plain old walking, has now become big business in America. The Walking Magazine has a circulation of more than 600,000. Some two hundred models of walking shoes are sold in shoe stores and sporting goods stores across the nation. Walking clubs are booming in popularity (see Appendix B for addresses of club headquarters). Walkers can be spotted striding along in most cities and towns. These exercisers tend to walk quite briskly, at a personally comfortable pace, with a determined swing of the arms. Whether they realize it or not, they are PaceWalking.

PACEWALKING PERKS

One of the biggest benefits of walking for exercise is that the activity is exceptionally safe and virtually injury free. Unlike jogging, which incurs the risk of muscle strains and sprains, shin splints and stress fractures, PaceWalking is a no- to low-risk sport. Joggers land hard, coming down with three to four times their body weight on each leg. Walkers land lightly with only one and a quarter times their body weight per step. So, unless you trip up due to lack of concentration or step out in front of a speeding car or bicyclist, your chances for injury are minimal. No pain, plenty of gain.

A PaceWalking program guarantees all of the benefits of aerobic exercise—physical, psychological, and spiritual. It can decrease your risk for heart attack and stroke. It can reduce high blood pressure and elevated blood cholesterol levels. It may minimize the risk for certain cancers, diabetes, arthritis, and other chronic diseases. And it may even prove to enhance the immune system, strengthening the body's natural self-protection system. By building stronger bones, it prevents or delays the onset of osteoporosis. PaceWalking your way to fitness can help to improve your circulation, speed up your digestive system, smooth out poor sleeping patterns, reduce chronic fatigue, even enhance your sex life! And like any aerobic exercise program, PaceWalking can help battle depression, boost your self-confidence, and increase your self-respect. (Exercisers are also less apt to be cigarette smokers or drug and alcohol abusers.) PaceWalking is a highly effective method for controlling stress. It can improve your disposition, clear your mind, relieve tension, and defuse bottled-up anger.

By utilizing calories directly, raising your metabolic rate and keeping it boosted, aerobic exercise is *the method of choice* for depleting fat stores. During the weight-loss process, regular exercise will preserve the lean muscle tissue that is lost with low-calorie diets. (For sedentary dieters who lose weight, up to 50 percent of the pounds shed may be precious muscle tissue!) And after weight loss, exercise helps to tighten and tone to prevent that unattractive "saggy" look.

As a real bonus, a regular exercise routine will act as an effective appetite suppressant! Plus, whenever you're out for a brisk walk, you're not home eating! PaceWalking, in combination with an adequate low-fat dietary intake, fights body fat—and wins!

WHEN TO SEE YOUR DOCTOR

It is sensible to consult your physician prior to beginning an exercise program. It is imperative to get your doctor's permission to exercise if you fit into any of the following categories:

- Diabetic
- Hypertensive or suffering from heart disease
- Arthritic or suffering from any other debilitating disease
- Over age fifty
- Pregnant

- Fifty-plus pounds overweight
- Chronic lung disease
- High blood cholesterol
- Cigarette smoker
- Sedentary lifestyle in recent years
- Take prescribed medication on a regular basis

Heavy people are at increased risk for orthopedic injury and joint discomfort. For the markedly overweight and those with chronic disease, intensive exercise may be prohibited. But oftentimes walking is allowed, even encouraged, as part of the treatment program.

HOW ACTIVE ARE YOU NOW?

Are you currently involved in a program of regular exercise, that is, running or jogging, bicycling, swimming, perhaps taking an aerobic dance class, or maybe even walking? If so, congratulations! You are already on the road to fitness, and you probably know how good it can feel *to feel good about yourself.* If you are currently content with your exercise routine, you may choose to continue with it. Or you may be looking for something new. Read on.

Are you burned out from your current exercise program, sick of pounding the pavement in your sweatpants, fed up with the chlorinated and crowded local pool? If you are bored or turned off by physical activity—past or present—PaceWalking may be for you.

Does the thought of donning a pair of running shorts or an aerobic dance leotard make you turn green, the idea of riding a bicycle send a chill of fear shooting up your spine? Do you worry that your busy lifestyle leaves you absolutely no time for exercise? The answer to your fears and hesitations: PaceWalking.

Let's take a close look at your current level of physical activity to see whether some changes may be warranted. Record the questions for the following Self-Evaluation: Moving It or Losing It? in your IDEAL Log. Be honest and accurate—that is, don't exaggerate the amount of exercise you are doing. The self-evaluation is just that—private and intended for you alone, useful as a means for self-reflection, self-understanding, and self-improvement. So if you're a sedentary couch potato (as I used to be), you might as well admit it. Your potential for improvement is phenomenal!

Self-Evaluation: Moving It or Losing It?

1. Do you currently engage in some sort of aerobic exercise (i.e., jogging, bicycling, swimming, aerobic dance, walking) for twenty minutes or more, three times a week or more? If so, describe the type of exercise you do, the average amount of time spent per exercise period, and the average number of exercise sessions per week.

2. Does your workday entail a *significant* amount of physical activity (for example, as a letter carrier, delivery person, house painter, construction worker, messenger, gym teacher)? If so, briefly describe your work and the type and degree of exercise involved.

3. Does your home life entail a *significant* amount of physical activity on a regular basis (for example, heavy gardening duties, lawn care, wood chopping, snow shoveling)? If so, briefly describe the type and duration of active work in which you are regularly engaged.

4. Do you ever commute all the way or part of the way to school or work by foot? If so, describe the length of your commute (in miles) and the average number of times per week that you walk this distance.

5. Do you *regularly* conduct errands, attend appointments, or make social visits on foot? If so, describe the typical length of your walks (in miles) and the average number of times per week that you travel by foot.

6. Of the sports listed below, which one(s) do you like? How often do you participate in any of these activities, if ever?

Aerobic dancing	Canoeing
Archery	Dancing—ballet, freestyle, modern
Badminton	Fencing
Baseball	Field hockey
Basketball	Figure skating
Bicycling	Football
Boxing	Golf

Gymnastics

Handball

Hiking

Horseback riding

Ice hockey

Martial arts—judo, karate, tai chi

Ping-pong

Racewalking

Racquetball

Rollerskating

Rowing

Running

Sailing

Skiing—cross country

Skiing—downhill

Snowshoeing

Soccer

Softball

Speedskating

Squash

Surfing

Swimming

Tennis

Track and field

Volleyball

Walking for exercise

Waterskiing

Weightlifting

7. Do you like spectator sports (for example, watching football on TV, attending softball games or professional baseball games)? If so, briefly describe your typical viewing behaviors (for example, "I watch the Knicks on TV every season and attend my son's Little League games all summer").

8. Do you watch television? If so, do you estimate your average number of viewing hours to be less than one hour a day? One to two hours a day? Two to three hours a day? Three to seven hours a day? Over seven hours a day?

Self-Analysis of Self-Evaluation:

1. An answer of "no" indicates that you are probably *not* fit and may need to incorporate a regular program of aerobic activity into your lifestyle.

2–5. The more "no" answers, the more sedentary your lifestyle.

6–7. You may *like* sports, but do you *do* any? Regularly? Think about why you may prefer spectator sports to participating in sports yourself.

8. Studies indicate that chronic television viewers tend to be more overweight than those who don't watch television or minimize their viewing habits. The average American's television set is on for over seven hours a day. It's no wonder the "average" American is also *overweight!*

FIT IN ONLY *THIRTY MINUTES* A DAY!

Can you spare one half-hour three (or more) days a week? Think about it: Do you often waste thirty minutes half-watching a television program you really have no interest in, half-listening to a phone call from someone you'd prefer not to be talking to, or half-dozing after dinner? Why lead your life half-heartedly? If you are willing to devote thirty minutes at least three days a week to your whole self, *PaceWalking can make you fit*. And if you are patient and persistent with your exercise plan, *PaceWalking can help you shed fat*. Fit not fat, in only thirty minutes a day, three to four times a week. Now, can you spare the time—for *you*?

Perhaps you are afraid that you will fail. I held this same fear for many years, so I didn't even try. But once I changed my mind-set, tackling the fear head on and simply going for it, I discovered that I had been wrong about myself all along! So give yourself the benefit of the doubt. *Get out of your own way,* and let the athlete within you emerge. PaceWalking is a doable, nonthreatening, fun way to begin.

Perhaps you are afraid of looking out of place, and this stops you from exercising. I remember feeling that way when I first pulled on my sweatpants. I felt that anyone who saw me would chuckle and think, "What's that fat guy trying to do, tripping along out there on the track?" Overweight people can be especially self-conscious and sensitive to critical eyes around them.

But the truth of the matter is that no one notices and nobody cares. These days, there are people of all ages, shapes, and sizes out on the trails. When they see you out there, too, they'll usually smile at you with empathy and encouragement. They know how you feel. They've been there, too. There's an intangible air of camaraderie within the fitness movement. So take a deep breath, and dare to take that first step. PaceWalking can make it easier for you to join the get-fit crowd.

An additional benefit of PaceWalking as an exercise choice is that the activity itself is less obvious and conspicuous than running or jogging. You may feel less awkward going out for a brisk walk than you would panting and puffing up and down the streets of your neighborhood. Yet the health-building and fat-burning benefits are the same. And *PaceWalking is fun!*

MAKING FITNESS FUN

Have you ever experienced the beauty and pleasure of a spring-time walk through a dappled park? Or enjoyed the fresh aroma of autumn's harvest during a walk through the woods? And have you noticed just how good your body feels when you go on a casual walk, flowing along smoothly and rhythmically, your arms swinging lightly, your breathing clean and deep? The act of walking is intrinsically enjoyable. And the feeling of being *in control of your body* can be exhilarating. Feeling good is, in and of itself, fun.

To add to your pleasure, PaceWalking outdoors on a nice day can offer a wide array of visual delights: flowers, babies, couples in love, sports cars, greenery, puppies . . . the list is endless. PaceWalking indoors at a shopping mall also provides plenty of interesting sights, from the store window wares to your fellow mall-walkers—and there are lots of them, as the practice has become quite popular, especially in areas where the climate can be especially humid or frigid. (Whenever the temperature is extreme, it may be best to exercise indoors, so if the thermometer tops 75 degrees or dips below 32 degrees, you may want to PaceWalk in the thermically controlled comfort of your local shopping mall.)

If you enjoy company while you exercise, find yourself a PaceWalking partner. An interesting discussion can make a thirty-minute walk appears to fly right by. And romance can blossom out on the walking trail! There are walking clubs sprouting up all across the country, so you may want to contact a national organization (see Appendix B) to find a local affiliate you can join.

The key to making fitness fun is to *enjoy the process*. Don't look at it as a form of self-punishment. Exercise is highly enjoyable, once you learn to like the feeling of moving your body, building muscles, and burning off fat.

EASY STEPS TO BIG CHANGES

Less than ten years ago, if you had informed me that I would one day enter and complete an Ironman distance triathlon, I would have questioned your sanity! I took the risk, I took the first step. Now look how far I've come! It all started with a brief walk-jog. My

friend Nancy transformed herself from a slightly overweight, totally sedentary executive to a slim, fit, daily fitness walker. She
doesn't compete in races, she PaceWalks on her own or with
friends—and loves it! Now *you* can do the same.

Do you want to walk away from your fears, to walk off your fat, to
walk your way to fitness? If you do, *you can!* Slowly, gradually, step
by step, you can PaceWalk yourself into a new, trim and fit you. In
the next chapter, I'll provide you with all of the practical information you need to become a PaceWalker, so that you can start *now.*

CHAPTER

5

How to PaceWalk— and Enjoy It!

Since PaceWalking the final stretch of the marathon in the 1985 Bud Light Endurance Triathlon on Cape Cod, I have PaceWalked several half-marathons, the 1987 and 1988 New York City Marathon, the entire marathon leg of the 1988 Bud Light Endurance Triathlon, and the run legs of several shorter triathlons. As a matter of fact, by the end of the 1988 racing season, I had given up running altogether, substituting PaceWalking for it entirely.

Of course, I still bike and swim for the triathlons. But PaceWalking is safe, sane, virtually pain-free, and just plain fun. And you can go pretty fast if you want to and work up your speed gradually. I'm getting my racing times down. I did the 1988 New York City Marathon in four hours and fifty-seven minutes, cutting an hour off my time in 1987. That's a pace of eleven minutes and 20 seconds. per mile. I did the first twenty miles at a pace of ten minutes and forty seconds per mile. The week before, I did a ten-kilometer race in fifty-two minutes and ten seconds—that's eight minutes and twenty-five seconds per mile. I can't *run* much faster than that.

Not only is it fun and can it be fast, but when you start PaceWalk-ing—whether simply for fun and fitness, or perhaps in competi-tion, as I have—you'll be pleased to discover that it's downright inexpensive as well!

SPORTS EQUIPMENT SAVVY

If you want to buy fancy gadgets and sportswear for extra incentive, by all means do so. But you don't have to. The only item you really need to purchase in order to begin PaceWalking is a good pair of shoes. Presently, only a few of the so-called "walking" shoes on the market are suitable for PaceWalking, even though they may work well for strolling or hiking. You may well find that running shoes will work better for PaceWalking.

First and foremost, the shoe must fit well; it should touch your foot in as many places as possible except over the toes. In other words, it should fit like a glove with no fingers, without pinching. The forefoot, the part that runs from the toe to the ball of your foot, should be very flexible. That will allow you to get a full follow-through with each step, as you come over your toes.

There should be a decent amount of cushioning under the heel. Your foot should feel firmly, snugly positioned *in* the shoe, not simply *on* it. To help achieve this, there should be a firm heel counter (the hard piece of material in the back of the shoe that goes around your heel). Foot movement within the shoe can lead to blisters and joint and muscle problems in the ankle and farther up the leg.

You should expect to pay at least $40 for a good pair of PaceWalking shoes. Walking and running shoes are reviewed periodically in the walking and running magazines. You may find the reviews to be helpful in making your selection.

PaceWalking clothing is something that you can spend a lot of money on, but you do not need to. If you cannot assemble the basic wardrobe from your closet and dresser, you can buy it for under $50. There are great modern fabrics, bright colors, and flattering styles available. But don't go overboard at first. Once you are certain that you are going to stick with PaceWalking, that you really like it, that you are not going to become a cyclist or a swimmer or an aerobic dancer instead, then you can wisely spend money on that spiffy-looking outfit you saw down at the sporting goods store.

Clothing should be loose-fitting and comfortable. I recommend wearing socks to help avoid blisters. For women I recommend a jogging bra. Men should wear support briefs or an athletic supporter. If you want to PaceWalk or run in cold weather, you will have to spend more money. For cold-weather workouts, several layers of light- to moderate-weight garments of a synthetic fabric that "breathes" are much better than one heavy-weight garment.

You should feel just a little on the chilly side when starting out. If you feel nice and toasty warm at the beginning of a PaceWalk on a cold day, you are sure to feel hot and uncomfortable well before the end of it. Avoid using old-fashioned heavy cotton sweats. They just keep moisture in. As this moisture condenses into water and falls onto your skin underneath those sweats, you will soon feel colder, not warmer.

You can buy an excellent digital stop watch for $20 to $35. Pick one that does not require a graduate degree in mechanical engineering in order to set it. Also, the buttons that you press to operate the stop watch function should be easy to reach with your finger.

You may want to PaceWalk with weights. It can be fun. It can also add to the vigor of your workout and help raise your heart rate into the aerobic range without requiring you to go faster. This is especially helpful for people who are already in reasonably good aerobic shape and may have to push it a bit to raise their heart rate above the aerobic minimum. PaceWalking with weights is perfectly safe, as long as you take the proper precautions. I like well-designed wrist and waist weights. I do not think that hand weights are a good idea. (Please see the technique section below for more information.)

Whatever you buy in the way of aerobic sports equipment, whether it be shoes, clothing, a bike, or a weight-training machine, buy it at a store that specializes in that kind of equipment so you are reasonably well assured of finding knowledgeable sales people. Only rarely will you find them in department stores. While general sporting goods stores—the kind that outfit local high school football teams—*may* have salespeople knowledgeable in running,

PaceWalking, or aerobic dance, you will find that is not always the case.

Most specialty stores are staffed by people who are aerobic athletes themselves. They can speak to you from personal experience, know about fit and function, and can intelligently interpret for you the comments of other users. In the end, of course, you will decide what looks and feels the best for you. In any store, if you feel that the person serving you really doesn't know what he or she is talking about, ask to see the manager. If none is available, go somewhere else.

ON THE SPOT

Small weights and various gadgets are marketed as "the latest" devices for reducing the excess fat found on specific body sites. "Thirty Minutes to Thin Your Thighs!" "Fifteen Seconds for a Flatter Stomach!" "Lose Those Love Handles in a Hurry!" The concept of stretching, lifting, rubbing, and rolling away those extra inches may sound plausible, certainly an appealing alternative to strenuous exercise, but the truth is *spot reducing does not work*.

During the weight-loss process, fat is lost at a fairly even rate from all over the body. *It is physiologically impossible* to diet and/ or exercise the fat away from one specific spot. And pounding, pummeling, massaging, or manipulating fat stores accomplishes nothing. Surgical liposuctioning can remove small amounts of body fat from buttocks, thighs, stomach, etc., but this is an expensive, painful, and risky procedure. The results are only temporary, unless (poor) eating and (non)exercise habits are altered to prevent fat regain.

Calisthenics and resistance training can tone muscles to improve appearance but will not directly reduce body fat. Doing a hundred sit-ups a day, for example, can build up certain muscles in the abdominal area, but the excess body fat will remain—unless an aerobic exercise program and a low-fat eating plan are also undertaken. And this, of course, is the ultimate solution to reducing body fat all over, including the specific spots of personal concern.

Cellulite serves as a common target for clever sales pitches promoting the marketing of a wide array of creams, wraps, and other gadgetry for "melting away" the lumpy fat. But cellulite is simply excess body fat. The wrinkled, puckered appearance is due to the stretching of connective tissue over the underlying fat stores. The only cure for cellulite is to improve muscle tone and to reduce body fat with a regular exercise routine and smart eating practices. Brisk walks will strengthen leg muscles, helping to tone the problem spots prone to cellulite/fat accumulation.

BODY BIORHYTHMS

Some people drag through the morning hours and perk up at night, while others are wide awake when the sun rises and asleep soon after it sets. With exercise, it is important to become familiar with the internal rhythms of your own body, so that you can take advantage of your high-energy times and avoid pushing yourself during low-energy periods. Women have to take into consideration their monthly cycle, in addition to daily cycles of energy (more on that in chapter 11).

I usually work out in the morning before going to work. That gives me a psychological boost that lasts all day. As far as fat loss is concerned, however, it is best to exercise at the end of the day, just before dinner. A brisk PaceWalk at five or six P.M. can really help to quell the appetite for the remainder of the evening (a big boon for us night eaters). One of my secretaries recently informed me that she now substitutes a midday PaceWalk for her former sedentary (and high-fat) lunch break, and she feels much more energetic upon returning to work. Test it out and see what works best for *you*.

A NOTE ON SAFETY

For most of us, late night walks through a deserted park—no matter how brisk the pace—may prove unwise, possibly downright dangerous. You know your own city or town. PaceWalk where and while it is most enjoyable—and safe.

Be defensive, and be aware. Watch out for traffic, speeding bicyclists and runners, and move out of the way if need be—quickly! Leave your wallet and your valuables at home. (I usually carry a few coins and an identification card in my pocket, certainly nothing worth taking.) And if you wear headphones, never use the ones that you stick right in your ear. Use the ones with the little foam cushions, and place them on your head *in front* of your ears. Then you will have a better chance of hearing an approaching automobile or an animal or other PaceWalker.

It is also important to *monitor yourself.* Don't push too hard, especially if you are older, seriously overweight, or in ill health. And be extra careful in the heat. Always work your way up slowly to a brisk pace of three and a half to four miles per hour—anything faster than this is more like a slow jog—and *slow down if you notice any of the following warning signs:*

- Rapid pulse (see heart rate chart on page 73)
- Sharp pain or cramps
- Chills or nausea
- Dizziness
- Excessive fatigue

Don't ever stop suddenly in the midst of your exercise routine. *Slow down to cool down.* Otherwise, the rapidly circulating blood can pool in your legs, causing weakness, dizziness, possibly fainting.

THE BENDS

Stretching before and after a walk will loosen up tight muscles and can help to prevent soreness and injury. For walkers, proper stretching beforehand provides the elasticity and mobility needed to keep hips, knees, and ankles flexible. After a walk, stretching is recommended to allow the feeling of flexibility to continue. But be careful not to stretch too rapidly nor to strain. And *don't bounce.* Stretch gently, slowly, just enough to loosen the muscles. For the seriously overweight, who are more prone to orthopedic problems and joint injuries, pre- and postwalk stretching is especially important for prevention purposes.

Be sure to stretch out the muscles you'll be exercising. For PaceWalkers, this means to do stretches designed for:

- Achilles tendons
- Calves
- Quadriceps
- Hamstrings
- Groin
- Back
- Arms and shoulders

For guidelines on proper stretching exercises and techniques, look in your local bookstore or library for an illustrated guidebook. My books *Triathloning for Ordinary Mortals* and *PaceWalking: The Balanced Way to Aerobic Health* have complete sections on stretching. Several other good reference resources are included in Appendix B.

THE ART OF PACEWALKING

PaceWalking is aerobic walking for sport, exercise, and health, at your own pace. It is a special form of ordinary walking, that motion of the body that everyone who is physically able uses as their primary means of getting around. But now walking is being used for aerobic exercise.

George Sheehan, M.D., the "guru" of running for health and fitness, had this to say about walking (in his "Running Wild" column in *The Physician and Sports Medicine* for October 1986): "Walking is the best exercise of all. It requires little or no instruction. . . . Walking is also virtually free of injury. . . . The body generally prefers walking to other exercise. . . . Walking is a gentle, effective way to become fit."

Aerobic walking will do for your body and your mind what any of the other aerobic sports will do when done at the same level of intensity for the same amount of time.

Fast walking as an aerobic sport goes by many names: "exercise walking," "fitness walking," "health walking," "power walking," "aerobic walking," "sportwalking," "striding." In 1985, I coined the term *PaceWalking*. I am pleased that it has caught on as one of the most common names for the sport.

PaceWalking is simple. Because it is technically easy as well as easy on the body, it is ideal for the IDEAL Exercise Plan. You walk fast with a purposeful stride of medium length. With each step, you land on your heel, roll forward along the outside of the foot, and push off your toes into the next step. Your back should be comfortably straight, not rigid. Your shoulders should be dropped and relaxed, your head up.

You swing your arms forward and back strongly, with your elbows comfortably bent. (Keeping your arms straight will just lead to an uncomfortable accumulation of fluid in your hands.) Don't swing your arms across your chest. That may look good and feel very vigorous, but it hinders your forward momentum. It also may lead to body imbalance and possible injury. Obviously, your right arm should go forward with your left leg and vice-versa. Your fingers should be lightly closed. You should never clench your fists.

On the foreswing, your hand should reach about to upper chest level. At the end of the backswing, you should feel a tug at the back of your shoulder. It is the combination of leg stride and arm swing that makes PaceWalking aerobic for most people, bringing two major muscle groups into play.

Your feet should point straight ahead. You should try to keep them as close as possible to an imaginary white line along which you walk. If you feel comfortable doing it, you can rotate your hip forward with the forward motion of the leg on the same side. This is something like racewalking. But hip rotation is certainly not essential. If it doesn't work for you, don't do it. I have PaceWalked quite a bit and do little hip rotation. Finally, one foot should always be in contact with the ground. That's what makes PaceWalking walking. It's also what sharply reduces the pounding, as compared with running or jogging.

In running and jogging you are airborne with each step. As you come down on the forward foot, all the weight of the body is borne by that foot. In PaceWalking, a significant portion of your weight is still on the rear foot as you come down on the front one. Hence, much less pressure, much more fun.

Balance, smoothness, rhythm, and lift are very important to an effective, comfortable, efficient PaceWalking gait. You should try to have as little extraneous body motion as possible. Nothing jerky. As you get into PaceWalking and become more comfortable with it, you will find that you can get a very nice lift with each step. You do this by making sure that you follow through all the way through each step. You land on your heel (not the sole or ball of your foot), roll forward along the outside of your foot, and then push off nicely with your toes. As you push off, you should bend your toes up just about as far as they can go. Once you have a nice rhythm, you will find that following through will add a lift to each step. This will further enhance the rhythm and make PaceWalking even more fun.

You will find it helpful if your breathing as well as your gait is rhythmic. When you first start walking in the IDEAL Exercise Plan, you will probably not be breathing hard. But as your stamina and proficiency increase, you will go faster. Both your rate and depth of breathing will increase. It is important to breathe deeply. You will bring in more oxygen and expel more carbon dioxide with each breath. Using your diaphragm and chest muscles to expand your lungs downward, while simultaneously expanding the rib-cage outward, will enable you to breathe as deeply as possible. (The diaphragm is the wide horizontal band of tissue that goes across the bottom of the lung cavity, separating it from the abdominal cavity. It moves downward with full lung expansion.)

As your speed and breathing rate pick up, you may well find it most comfortable to link your breathing with your steps. For example, you might breathe in for three paces, then out for three paces. Rhythmic breathing will help establish the overall rhythm, smoothness, and balance that make PaceWalking so pleasurable.

Stride length will vary from person to person, and you may well find yours changing during your workouts. For example, you will most likely alter your stride length with the terrain, taking longer steps when you are going downhill, shorter ones when you are going uphill. On level ground, the shorter your stride, the faster you can move your legs. A longer stride will require a greater expenditure of muscle energy for each step, but there will be fewer steps per unit of time. Either method can produce an aerobic heart rate (see chapter 6). In PaceWalking, that's what's critical, not stride length *per se*. Do be careful not to overstride and hurt yourself.

As to PaceWalking with weights, you can safely carry them on your wrists, waist, and ankles. Wrist weights are rings that slide over your hand and then snug up on your lower forearm. I like the kind that start you off with a half-pound on each wrist. They are easy to get used to, safe, and comfortable. Light weights will not interfere with your nice, smooth rhythm or distort your arm swing.

Even after you get used to wrist weights, for safety I think that it is a good idea to stop at two pounds. In any case, you cannot do body building by walking with wrist or hand weights.

You can safely carry waist weights up to a maximum of about twenty pounds, provided the weight carrier is designed to position the weights at your sides, over your hips. Carrying weights on your abdomen or lower back can cause postural distortion and injury. Some people like ankle weights. Very light ones (start with a half-pound, up to a maximum of two) can be used safely as long as you are sensitive to any unusual pains that develop and you respond appropriately.

I do not recommend PaceWalking with weights in a backpack. In that position, the weight can constrict both your breathing and your arm movement, and distort your posture, leading to injury. Nor do I recommend hand weights. Squeezing your fingers around the handles increases tension in your upper body and may cause an increase in blood pressure. In PaceWalking, you should be relaxed, not tense. Also, if you lose your grip, the weight could fly out of your hand, causing you or a companion injury.

PACEWALKING IS IDEAL FOR *YOU*

For the majority of older people, walking is the easiest, safest, most desirable form of exercise. This often holds true for over-weight people as well. Since it is practical and can be so enjoyable, most people find it possible to adopt and *stay on* a walking pro-gram. And this makes PaceWalking the ideal activity for losing excess body fat and controlling weight. PaceWalking can be a natural, healthful, enjoyable addition to most anyone's lifestyle.

6

The IDEAL Exercise Plan: Phases I, II, III

The IDEAL Exercise Plan is a graduated walking program, provided here in three separate phases. Based on your current level of fitness, age, degree of overweight, and amount of time available, you can begin with the phase appropriate for you. Then you can personalize your exercise plan to suit your individual lifestyle patterns. Eventually, as your fitness and motivation increase, you can—if you choose to—move on to the next phase.

If you are a nonexerciser, a novice PaceWalker, or otherwise interested in starting up slowly, Phase I of the IDEAL Exercise Plan is for you. You begin very simply with a ten-minute walk three days a week.

For regular exercisers, Phase II may be a more appropriate level of physical activity. Read through each phase to determine which best suits your own needs, habits, and physical condition. Start slowly and progress gradually.

AEROBIC AND NONAEROBIC EXERCISE

Most people who exercise on a regular basis do aerobic exercise. *Aerobic exercise* (a term coined by Dr. Kenneth Cooper in the

1960s), uses oxygen in breathed-in air as its primary energy source. Aerobic exercise means that your muscles are "taking up," that is using, an increased amount of oxygen over what they normally use.

Now remember, exercise does not have to be aerobic to be beneficial for weight and fat loss. Any kind of increased muscular activity will burn extra calories stored in fat. It will also set your resting metabolic rate back up. So don't think that on the first day you have to get out there and be ready to huff and puff and sweat and get your heart rate up. Actually, if you haven't exercised in a long time, that's the worst thing you can do. But if your exercise eventually becomes aerobic, you will get more out of it.

Starting from scratch, you just want to get out and walk for ten minutes or so three times a week, for a couple of weeks. Just begin to get used to the idea of exercising on a regular basis. That's the first step: getting into the habit of setting aside time for exercise on a regular basis. It is likely you will find that just doing that will make you feel good. You have begun to take control, to take responsibility. You are doing something new and different that's going to help you achieve goals that you really want to achieve, for yourself. Don't worry about speed, time, or distance at the beginning. Getting on a regular schedule is a big enough challenge for the previously sedentary person or the long-lapsed exerciser. Once you begin, you will go longer, farther, and faster soon enough.

Don't worry about aerobics right away, either. You may never become an aerobic exerciser, remaining just an exerciser. What's important is what works for you. But if you do stick with it, the likelihood is that your exercise will become aerobic. And then you will not only get an increased rate of fat burning, but you will also get all of the other health benefits that go along with aerobic, as contrasted with nonaerobic, exercise.

How do we know when we are exercising aerobically? Well, for the healthy person without heart disease, nature provides a good measurement of muscle oxygen uptake that is simple for anyone to take. That measurement is the heart rate. Exercise physiology has determined that when your heart rate rises above a certain level, you are doing aerobic exercise.

There is a simple formula for finding out what that level is. First, you subtract your age from the number 220. The exercise phys-

iologists call the result the *theoretical maximum heart rate*. Then
you calculate 70 percent of 220 minus your age. That figure is the
minimum heart rate that you need to achieve if the exercise that
you are doing is to qualify as aerobic.

To be on the safe side, you should never go above 85 percent of
your theoretical max. If you find that your heart rate exceeds your
theoretical max, you are working your body too hard. Slow down
gradually, and cool down gradually. If you don't feel well after
having cooled down, see your doctor. *If your heart rate consistently runs high or you feel palpitations in your chest or pain in
your chest, arms, or jaw, you may be experiencing the symptoms
of heart disease. Stop working out until you can see a doctor.*

Thus for aerobic exercise, your so-called *target zone* is 70 to 85
percent of 220 minus your age. The accompanying Heart Rate
Chart shows the target heart rates (THR) for some sample ages.

HEART RATE CHART

Age	Healthy Aerobic Heart Rate	Maximum Heart Rate
20	140–170	200
25	136–166	195
30	133–162	190
35	130–157	185
40	126–153	180
45	122–149	175
50	119–144	170
55	116–140	165
60	112–136	160
65	108–132	155

How do you find out what your heart rate is? You've seen
doctors and nurses taking the pulse at the wrist. Out on the road
there is a much easier way to do it. At the side of your neck there is
a thick band of muscle that runs from the notch at the back of your
upper jaw to the notch that marks the middle of your collar-bone.

Feel along the front border of this muscle band with your index and middle fingers. About halfway down you will come across a large pulsating blood vessel, the carotid artery. You should be able to find it fairly easily. If you cannot, try using the other hand. (By the way, don't try to find it and press on it on both sides of your neck at the same time. You could cause yourself to pass out. If you have any suspicion that you have arteriosclerosis, hardening of the arteries—or any disease of the blood vessels in the neck—take your pulse at the wrist, on the thumb side, the way doctors and nurses do.)

Once you find your pulse in your neck, you will need a digital watch or one with a second hand to determine your heart rate. Counting the first beat as zero, you count for five seconds and multiply by 12, six seconds and multiply by 10, or fifteen seconds and multiply by 4. Use whichever multiplication table you are most comfortable with. The longer you count, the more accurate your measurement will be. You will know instantly if you are exercising intensely enough to get your heart rate up into the aerobic range.

THE IDEAL EXERCISE PLAN: INTRODUCTION

The IDEAL Exercise Plan has three phases. The first *introduces* you to regular exercise. The second *develops* your skills and abilities as an IDEAL exerciser. The third shows you three levels of *maintenance* for the new you. You can pick one to stay with, alternate among two of them, or rotate among all three. The choice is yours.

Many people will want to start gradually, with Phase I. If you are markedly overweight, over age fifty, pregnant, suffering from a chronic disease, and/or limited in your physical abilities, you should certainly start with Phase I. However, if you have had some exercise experience or get off to a quick start, there's no reason why you cannot move to Phase II right away.

THE PROGRAMS

Each program is thirteen weeks long and has three to five workouts scheduled per week. All workouts are measured in minutes, not miles. That is because it's time, not speed or distance that counts for both weight loss and aerobic health. Also, having workouts in minutes makes it much easier to pick out courses: out fifteen minutes and back fifteen minutes. There's no measuring course lengths with the car.

The tables show you how many minutes you should do for each workout. Don't feel that you must follow the programs rigidly. They are guides, not requirements. You can make changes to suit your own needs and schedule, as long as you generally stay within the IDEAL exercise principles. In other words, don't do your two hours per week by taking one very long PaceWalk each Sunday. That won't help you lose weight or fat, it won't improve your aerobic fitness status, and it may lead to injury. If you miss a session and feel that you would like to make up the time (which you certainly do not have to do for the occasional miss), don't do so all at once. Spread out the make-up minutes over several workout sessions.

It will not hurt to do two workouts in a row during the week. If bad weather or travel or an early morning meeting causes you to miss a Tuesday, you can do that workout on Wednesday and still do your Thursday workout as well. It won't hurt to do your workouts at different times on different days. I usually work out in the morning. But if on a particular day I find it more convenient to work out in the evening, I do. This happens especially when I am traveling.

The three phases connect with each other in a logical manner, just as the three phases of the IDEAL Eating Plan do. At the end of Phase I, you'll be doing one and a half hours per week. Phase II, the development phase, gets you all the way up to three hours per week. For Phase III, maintenance, I give you a choice of levels: two, three, or four hours per week.

EXERCISE, HEALTH, AND FITNESS

None of the programs go above three hours per week except "Maintenance Double Plus" in Phase III. If you are exercising aerobically, three hours per week are all you need on a long-term basis to get the maximum health benefit from your efforts.

Health is a state of well-being, optimum functioning, the absence of disease, and the control of both external and internal risk factors for disease. The American College of Sports Medicine has concluded that the minimum exercise program needed to provide some improvement in health is twenty minutes three to four times per week. Dr. Cooper has found that you get increasing health benefits from increasing aerobic exercise, up to a level of two and a half to three hours per week.

Fitness is the ability to do physical work over time using the musculo-skeletal and cardiovascular systems. Fitness does improve over the two-and-a-half-to-three-hour per week figure. But improved fitness is only really needed by athletes. As Dr. Cooper says, anyone who is aerobically exercising for more than three hours per week is doing it for reasons other than health protection and improvement. That's why my programs here generally stop at three hours. (If you want to go on and do some racing, which requires improved fitness, see the chapter on racing in my book *PaceWalking: The Balanced Way to Aerobic Health,* or refer to my book *Triathloning for Ordinary Mortals.*)

THE IDEAL EXERCISE PLAN: PHASE I

These are your *exercise goals:*

- To get in the habit of being a regular exerciser, to make regular exercise a part of your life
- To get used to the sport or sports that you have chosen for your program
- Assuming that you are exercising aerobically, to get up and over the "aerobic minimum" level, twenty minutes, three times per week

The *Introductory Program* (see accompanying table) has three workouts per week. It starts at thirty minutes for the week and finishes at an hour and a half for the week. As I said above, if you've never done any aerobic exercise, or haven't for a long time, I suggest that you begin here. I've designed this program to ease you into a regular schedule of workouts gradually, to help you limber up.

IDEAL EXERCISE PLAN: PHASE I
Introductory Program

Week	M	T	W	Th	F	Sa	S	Total
				(times in minutes)				
1	Off	10	Off	10	Off	Off	10	30
2	Off	10	Off	10	Off	Off	10	30
3	Off	20	Off	20	Off	Off	20	60
4	Off	20	Off	20	Off	Off	20	60
5	Off	20	Off	20	Off	Off	20	60
6	Off	20	Off	20	Off	Off	20	60
7	Off	20	Off	20	Off	Off	30	70
8	Off	20	Off	20	Off	Off	30	70
9	Off	20	Off	20	Off	Off	20	60
10	Off	20	Off	20	Off	Off	30	70
11	Off	20	Off	30	Off	Off	30	80
12	Off	20	Off	30	Off	Off	30	80
13	Off	30	Off	30	Off	Off	30	90

Comments:
   Weeks 1–4: Walk at your usual, ordinary pace.
   Weeks 5–8: Walk at a fast pace.
   Weeks 9–13: PaceWalk!

THE FIRST TWO WEEKS

For the first two weeks, you will be going out for just a ten-minute walk three times each week. Walk at a comfortable pace for the ten minutes, or a bit longer if you feel like it. For many people starting out to become regular exercisers, it's the regularity that's the hardest part. So at the beginning, I give you nothing else to do but become regular—to get that schedule into your calendar and stick to it. The objective is to get you up a bit earlier in the morning, to get you out of bed when you might not be quite ready to do so, have you put on your PaceWalking outfit and go out just to walk—and to do it even if the weather isn't quite right.

This is your chance to get in control and stay in control, right away. You have a first crack at immediate gratification, although it's not the kind you're used to with those quick-loss diets. On this plan you won't lose twenty pounds in two weeks—I can almost guarantee you that. It's not that kind of gratification that I'm talking about. It's gratification of the mind.

In two weeks you can take control of your life, adding something new that will help you to become the new you that you want to be. In two weeks, you can take the first big step toward making regular exercise a part of your life. In two weeks you can show yourself that you are ready to take responsibility for the way you look, the way you feel, and the way you feel about yourself. That will give you gratification aplenty.

WEEKS TWO THROUGH FOUR

For the next two weeks, you will go out for twenty minutes at a time, still just walking at a comfortable pace. You will continue your loosening-up process and continue getting used to being on a schedule of workouts, while doubling the time that you spend. As your workouts increase in length, you can begin exploring different routes that you will use later.

WEEKS FIVE THROUGH NINE

In weeks five through eight, you are still just walking, but you begin to pick up the pace. I'm not talking about PaceWalking here. You do not have to take your pulse, although you may want to out of curiosity. Don't worry about your arm swing; just try for smoothness and comfort while walking fast. Don't worry about walking technique either, but do work on developing a steady, smooth, easy rhythm to your walking. Rhythm makes walking fun, easy, and prepares you for PaceWalking.

In week nine, you begin to PaceWalk. Take a look again at the section on technique in chapter 5. Don't worry about all the details. Just focus on the following four points: relaxed upper body, no scrunched shoulders; strong arm swing; firm heelstrike, rolling forward to a nice, lifting push-off from your toes; smooth, steady rhythm—rockin', rollin', and liftin'. And don't worry about speed.

Take your pulse halfway through and at the end of each work-out. You will probably find yourself above the 70 percent figure, in the aerobic range. If not, don't worry about it. As you speed up your pace, and especially as you accentuate and strengthen your arm swing, your heart rate will get up there. A good rate to aim at is 70 to 75 percent of 220 minus your age.

FINISHING PHASE I

The balance of the Introductory Program is spent PaceWalking. You should use this time to work on technique. You still don't have to worry about speed, except for keeping your heart rate elevated if you've decided to do aerobic rather than nonaerobic exercise. You will become more comfortable with the gait. You will also really be incorporating regular exercise into your lifestyle.

WHAT YOU'VE DONE

Before the end of the thirteen weeks, almost everyone who undertakes this regimen will see and feel results. Since you are combining the Ideal Exercise Plan with the Ideal Eating Plan, you will have lost some weight and fat. For the woman of average height who is twenty or more pounds above her desired weight, the weight loss will probably be in the ten-to-fifteen-pound range. That may not sound like a lot, but if you follow my advice on eating and exercise, those are pounds that will *stay* off, unlike so many of those pounds people lose on fad diets, which sneak right back on after you stop dieting.

You will look better. Not only will you have lost weight, you will probably also have redistributed some of the remaining pounds by losing fat and adding some muscle. As I continue to exercise and continue to build muscle and lose fat, my weight remains fairly constant—between about 175 in the summer and 180 in the winter. To this day, people who haven't seen me in a while often say, "You've really lost weight!" I have to tell them that I haven't lost weight, but that I have substituted trim muscle for flabby fat. You will likely feel better and feel better about yourself after completing the thirteen weeks. As Dr. George Sheehan puts it, you will gain in "energy, clarity, and self-esteem."

The Introductory Program is purposely designed to provide a slow and easy introduction to PaceWalking, or to any of the other sports you may choose. However, if you find it goes too slowly for you, don't feel constrained to follow it minute by minute, day by day, and week by week. Add minutes, add workouts, and/or skip the early weeks of ordinary walking if you feel that you don't need them. Some people become very enthusiastic very early on and move ahead very quickly. If that is right for you, fine. But do *be careful not to overdo it.*

THE IDEAL EXERCISE PLAN: PHASE II

These are your exercise goals:

- To establish a firm pattern of regular exercise as part of your life
- To work up to the "aerobic max" of three hours per week of regular exercise

Phase II, the *Developmental Program,* has four workouts per week, starting in week three. Two are on weekdays, and two are on weekend days. It's more demanding than Phase I. Yet in every week, one-half or more of the total minutes are on the two weekend days. This makes life easier for the working IDEAL exerciser.

This phase will develop your regular exercise to the point where you are doing two to three hours per week. If you've followed the schedule as given, at the end of Phase II you will have been on an exercise schedule for twenty-six weeks. For most people that means that exercise has become a regular part of their life and that they should be able to continue a regular exercise program indefinitely—that is, unless they set unrealistic goals and did too much, too soon, and got injured, angry, or frustrated, or they were not internally motivated and became tired, bored, and ridden with guilt feelings.

This phase begins with a week off. You will see in Phase III that I regularly schedule time off, every thirteen weeks. This gives your mind and body some rest. Don't worry. You won't lose your conditioning. Your blossoming new shape will certainly not revert to pre-IDEAL in a week, as long as you stick with your IDEAL

IDEAL EXERCISE PLAN: PHASE II
Developmental Program

Week	M	T	W	Th	F	Sa	S	Total
				(times in minutes)				
1	Off	Off	Off	Off	Off	Off	Off	Off
2	Off	20	Off	20	Off	Off	20	60
3	Off	20	Off	20	Off	20	20	80
4	Off	20	Off	20	Off	20	30	90
5	Off	20	Off	30	Off	20	30	100
6	Off	20	Off	30	Off	20	40	110
7	Off	30	Off	30	Off	30	30	120
8	Off	30	Off	30	Off	30	40	130
9	Off	30	Off	40	Off	30	40	140
10	Off	30	Off	40	Off	30	50	150
11	Off	40	Off	30	Off	30	60	160
12	Off	40	Off	30	Off	40	60	170
13	Off	30	Off	40	Off	50	60	180

Eating Plan. By taking a week off in the IDEAL Exercise Plan, you are preventing *exercise burnout.*

After the week off, there is a light week, in time well below the last one of the Introductory Program. After that the weekly time requirement begins to build again, which it does steadily throughout this program. Notice how the workout lengths vary within each week, following the "hard-easy" principle that is now ingrained in endurance sports training worldwide.

The Developmental Program "maxes out" at three hours. Virtually anyone can safely and comfortably get to that level. However, if you know in advance that you are going to use the Maintenance Program rather than one of the other programs in Phase III, you do not have to get to that level. In that case, go through week nine and then do weeks six through nine again, substituting them for weeks nine through thirteen.

In either case, you will be using the latter part of the program to get your technique down and your speed up. You will be getting into better shape than you have ever been in. You will probably find that in order to boost your heart rate above the aerobic minimum you will have to work harder. In PaceWalking, you will see how important that arm swing really is.

When you finish the Developmental Program, congratulate yourself. You have become a regular exerciser. You are becoming aerobically fit and healthy. Your stamina and endurance will have increased markedly. You may have discovered that you are talented in sports. That will open up whole new vistas for you.

You will have lost weight and, by losing fat, have redistributed some of your remaining weight. You are feeling better and feeling better about yourself. Reward yourself. Go out and buy that great sports outfit you have been eyeing. Get away for a special weekend in the country, with or without exercise as a part of it. Or, dare I say it, have that double hot-fudge sundae that you have been dutifully putting off for the last three months. (Actually, make it a single. A double has too much fat. Now that you are a low-fat eater, you will just feel rotten afterward if you eat too much of it.)

THE IDEAL EXERCISE PLAN: PHASE III

These are your *exercise goals:*

- To confirm your commitment to regular exercise
- To settle upon the maintenance program that is going to work for you
- To become comfortable with and skilled in the sport or sports that you have selected for your IDEAL Exercise Plan

You've made it! Six months ago you decided that the internal motivation was there, that you were going to make regular exercise a part of your life. You've lost weight and fat. You look better, you feel better, and you feel better about yourself. You took control of your life. You took responsibility for your shape. You stopped playing victim, you stopped making excuses, you stopped putting your fitness program off until tomorrow, you got over your fear of failure, you may well also have had to overcome fear of success. You went out and did it!

And just what is it that you've done in addition to becoming a regular exerciser? If you've settled on aerobic exercise, you've worked yourself into reasonably good aerobic shape. Gradually, slowly, but steadily, you've worked your way up to three hours per week. That's the equivalent of fifteen to twenty miles of running per week, more than the average American runner does. You may have begun to open up some vistas in sport that you didn't even know were on your personal horizon. You're now ready for Phase III of the IDEAL Exercise Plan, maintenance.

In this phase, you have three different maintenance choices for your IDEAL Exercise Plan: Maintenance, Maintenance Plus, and Maintenance Double-Plus. In Maintenance you work out every other day. That's three days one week, four the next. Your total time is two hours per week. Maintenance Plus gives you four days per week, for a total of three hours. Maintenance Double-Plus gives you five days per week for a total of four hours. You also have the option of changing off among the maintenance programs from quarter to quarter.

In the Maintenance Program, you begin again with a week off. Rest, relax, feel good about yourself. Then you will get going again. Many regular exercisers find two hours per week a comfortable, productive amount. You may as well. The every-other-day schedule has been standard among weight-lifters for years. Since there is only one weekend day of PaceWalking per week in this program, it is impossible to concentrate the workout minutes on the weekends. But the program is nicely balanced. There is no weekday workout of more than 40 minutes, with the average being about 30.

The Maintenance Plus Program provides you with an average of three hours of aerobic exercise per week for the twelve weeks of the program that follow the obligatory first week off. You can go into Maintenance Plus directly from Phase II.

There are four workouts per week in the Maintenance Plus Program. More than half the total minutes are concentrated in the two weekend days. The three-hour figure comes, of course, from the "three-hour max" that I mentioned earlier. Many IDEAL exercisers will find this to be a very comfortable permanent program.

IDEAL EXERCISE PLAN: PHASE III
Maintenance Program

(times in minutes)

Week	M	T	W	Th	F	Sa	S	Total
1	Off	Off	Off	Off	Off	Off	Off	Off
2	Off	30	Off	30	Off	40	Off	100
3	30	Off	40	Off	20	Off	40	130
4	Off	40	Off	30	Off	40	Off	110
5	30	Off	40	Off	20	Off	40	130
6	Off	40	Off	30	Off	60	Off	130
7	20	Off	30	Off	30	Off	40	120
8	Off	40	Off	30	Off	50	Off	120
9	20	Off	40	Off	20	Off	60	140
10	Off	30	Off	30	Off	40	Off	100
11	20	Off	30	Off	20	Off	40	110
12	Off	40	Off	30	Off	60	Off	130
13	20	Off	30	Off	30	Off	40	120

IDEAL EXERCISE PLAN: PHASE III
Maintenance Plus Program

(times in minutes)

Week	M	T	W	Th	F	Sa	S	Total
1	Off	Off	Off	Off	Off	Off	Off	Off
2	Off	30	Off	40	Off	30	50	150
3	Off	30	Off	50	Off	40	60	180
4	Off	40	Off	40	Off	50	80	210
5	Off	30	Off	50	Off	40	60	180
6	Off	50	Off	30	Off	50	70	200
7	Off	40	Off	30	Off	30	60	160
8	Off	30	Off	50	Off	40	60	180
9	off	30	Off	40	Off	30	50	150
10	Off	30	Off	50	Off	40	50	170
11	Off	40	Off	30	Off	50	70	190
12	Off	40	Off	40	Off	50	80	210
13	Off	30	Off	50	Off	40	60	180

IDEAL EXERCISE PLAN: PHASE III
Maintenance Double-Plus Program

(times in minutes)

Week	M	T	W	Th	F	Sa	S	Total
1	Off	Off	Off	Off	Off	Off	Off	Off
2	Off	30	40	Off	30	40	70	210
3	Off	30	50	Off	40	50	70	240
4	Off	40	40	Off	50	60	80	270
5	Off	30	50	Off	30	50	80	240
6	Off	50	30	Off	30	60	90	260
7	Off	40	30	Off	30	50	70	220
8	Off	30	50	Off	30	60	70	240
9	Off	30	40	Off	30	50	60	210
10	Off	30	50	Off	30	60	70	230
11	Off	40	30	Off	40	60	80	250
12	Off	40	40	Off	40	60	90	270
13	Off	30	50	Off	30	70	60	240

The Maintenance Double-Plus Program provides you with an average of four hours per week, spread over five workouts. You certainly could modify this to do the four hours in just four workouts if you like. If one hour is a comfortable workout time for you, just do four of those a week. If you prefer to vary your time week by week, as otherwise suggested, take one of the five sessions for that week in Maintenance Double-Plus, divide by four, and add the minutes to each of the remaining four workouts.

If you are working out aerobically, this program is the equivalent of about twenty-five miles per week of running. You are really getting up there. If you like this one, you have obviously become hooked on regular exercise. Aren't positive addictions wonderful? You may also have found that you really like aerobic sport for its own sake, not just for what it does for your mind and your body.

ADDING IN OTHER ACTIVITIES

Once you overcome your personal fitness hurdles and adopt the Ideal Exercise Plan, you should find that you really miss it on the days when you don't PaceWalk. But to add some variety to your exercise routine, you may want to incorporate one or more additional activities. Some PaceWalkers alternate their daily walks with running. Bicycling may require an initial financial investment in a good-quality ten- or twelve-speed bike and the proper shoes, but it can become a lifelong pastime. If you have access to a pool, you may want to work one or more swims into your weekly exercise plan. And if there is a local health club you would feel comfortable joining, low-impact aerobics and circuit weight training can serve as excellent forms of aerobic exercise, providing you with companionship, professional supervision, muscle toning, and fun. Remember, the exercise minutes in the IDEAL Exercise Plan tables are all interchangeable. Just mix and match in the way that works best for you.

WALKING MORE, NATURALLY

Even after you have adopted the exercise plan and have begun PaceWalking regularly, you may want to work in some additional mileage. The following list provides some practical tips for increasing the amount of time you spend on the move—painlessly, efficiently, and eventually habitually, when living a physically active lifestyle is totally natural for you. You will not be PaceWalking in these activities, but they will help you.

On the Move

- When doing errands or attending appointments, park your car or get off the bus several blocks away from your destination and walk the rest of the way—briskly.
- When traveling a short distance, walk there—briskly.
- Use your coffee break to go for a quick walk. (It'll help get you away from the doughnuts!)
- Use the first part of your lunch hour to go for a brisk walk. (It'll help to quell your appetite for lunch.)
- Opt for the stairs in place of the elevator or escalator, or ride part way and walk the rest.
- Take the dog for quick daily walks. (If you don't have a dog, borrow your neighbor's pet.)
- Instead of having the daily newspaper delivered to your door, walk to the local newsstand—briskly.
- Instead of driving to the post office, walk to a neighborhood mailbox—briskly.
- Walk to work or school, or get off public transportation a mile or so from your destination and walk the rest of the way— briskly.
- Walk home from work or school, or get off public transportation a mile or so from your destination and walk the rest of the way—briskly.
- Visit your neighbors and local friends on foot (but you might want to call ahead and warn them of your impending arrival).

EATING TO WIN

But won't your new exercise plan increase your nutritional needs? Won't all that PaceWalking build muscles and thus elevate your protein requirements? And should you stock up on special "athletic packs" of vitamins and minerals? What about carbohydrate loading before a road race; what about replacing lost fluids with "sports drinks" afterward?

Relax! Your nutrient requirements are not going to change in any significant way:

- You will be utilizing more *calories* as you PaceWalk each day, but your food intake will be adequate in energy value to meet your needs while allowing for gradual weight loss.
- Your *protein* intake will be ample but not overgenerous, as your need for this nutrient does not increase with a moderate muscle building and toning exercise program.
- Most sports nutritionists no longer advise athletes to embark on special *carbohydrate* loading diets, but you can be assured that the IDEAL Eating Plan provided in the next chapter will provide you with plenty of energy-stoking complex carbohydrates, foods rich in starches and fiber.
- And don't fall for the advertising lures that claim you will need to take *vitamin and mineral* supplements after exercising, as a well-balanced diet safely covers your needs for all nutrients. (An exception may be iron, especially in menstruating women. Special dietary guidance for this group is included in chapter 11.)

Research on the nutritional needs of nonprofessional athletes and active healthy persons has been limited. However, most sports nutritionists agree that the only significant dietary alteration required when you exercise is an adjustment in your *water* intake. When you are exercising, thirst is not a reliable guide to fluid replenishment. You will usually quench your thirst long before you have consumed enough fluid to replace your losses.

In order to prevent dehydration, be sure to drink at least two glasses of water several hours before you plan to exercise; then, drink one to two cups around fifteen minutes before you begin. Afterward, drink at least two cups more. When you exercise for longer than thirty minutes or if the weather is hot and humid, try to drink one cup of water every fifteen minutes during physical activity. Older people are especially susceptible to dehydration and should be exceedingly careful to replenish fluid losses. Everyone who is active should keep in mind the fact that dehydration not only hampers exercise performance and leads to cramps and fatigue, it can pose serious health problems and cause life-threatening side effects.

So be sure to drink up—before you PaceWalk and immediately afterward. And drink fluids *during* your PaceWalk whenever you're out for a long walk and on warm muggy days. There is no need to purchase special "sports drinks" unless you prefer them. Plain cool (40 to 50 degrees Fahrenheit) water is the ideal fluid choice. If you want to vary your beverage intake, be sure to dilute fruit juices and sweetened sports drinks with water. The high sugar content of undiluted juices and sugar-sweetened drinks can cause stomach cramps, as can carbonation, so avoid fizzy drinks, too.

Use the list that follows in order to select your fluid replacements wisely. Eat (and drink) to win at health for the active person—you!

CHOOSING THE IDEAL BEVERAGE

	Beverage	Ounces	Calories	Worth Noting
Coffee and tea:	Coffee, black	6	5	Contains 70–215 mg. caffeine
	Coffee, decaffeinated	6	2	Contains 2–6 mg. caffeine
	Tea, black	6	2	Contains 25–135 mg. caffeine (unless decaffeinated)
	Iced tea, sweetened	8	60–90	Contains 30–35 mg. caffeine, plus sugar
Fruit juices and drinks:	Apple juice	6	90	Not a significant source of vitamin C unless fortified
	Grape juice	6	120	May be fortified with vitamin C
	Grapefruit juice	6	70	Contains around 75 mg. vitamin C

	Beverage	Ounces	Calories	Worth Noting
	Grapefruit-orange juice	6	80	Contains around 75 mg. vitamin C
	Orange juice	6	85	Contains around 75 mg. vitamin C
	Pineapple juice	6	105	Contains around 60 mg. vitamin C
	Cranberry cocktail	6	110	Contains more than 6 tsp. sugar
	Fruit drinks	6	100	Approximately 5 tsp. sugar
	Fruit punch	6	85	Approximately 5 tsp. sugar
	Lemonade	6	75	Approximately 5 tsp. sugar
	Tang	8	120	Approximately 8 tsp. sugar
Milk and milk drinks:	Milk, skim	8	85	Contains less than 1 gram fat, 300 mg. calcium
	Milk, low-fat (1%)	8	105	Contains 3 grams fat, 300 mg. calcium
	Milk, low-fat (2%)	8	125	Contains 5 grams fat, 300 mg. calcium
	Milk, whole (3.5%)	8	150	Contains 8 grams fat (or 50% of total calories), 290 mg. calcium
	Milk, chocolate (3.5%)	8	210	Contains 8.5 grams fat, 280 mg. calcium, plus sugar
	Milkshake, chocolate	12	450	Contains 10 grams fat, 450 mg. calcium, plus 13 tsp. sugar
	Yogurt-fruit drinks	12	100	Contain 3 grams fat, fruit juice, no added sugar
	Liquid yogurts	8	180	Contain 2 grams fat, sugar and corn sweeteners

	Beverage	Ounces	Calories	Worth Noting
	Hot chocolate	6	110	Approximately 3 tsp. sugar
	Hot chocolate, sugar-free	6	50	Contains artificial sweeteners
	Instant breakfast, chocolate	8	280	Contains 6 tsp. sugar, 9 grams fat (unless made with skim milk)
Soft drinks and mixers:	Club soda	12	0	May contain 40–75 mg. sodium
	Diet soft drinks	12	0–30	Contain artificial sweeteners, up to 45 mg. caffeine
	Seltzers	12	0–135	Plain or with essence of fruit preferable to brands sweetened with corn syrup
	Ginger ale	12	80	Approximately 5 tsp. sugar
	Root beer	12	100	Approximately 7 tsp. sugar
	Tonic water	12	115	Sweetened with sugar or corn syrup
	Cola	12	160	Approximately 10 tsp. sugar, up to 60 mg. caffeine
Sports drinks:	Gatorade	12	75	Contains half the sugar of fruit drinks
	Exceed	12	105	Made with hydrolyzed corn starch, fructose, and minerals (including sodium for 75 mg. per serving), plus artificial color and flavor; useful in endurance exercise only

Beverage	Ounces	Calories	Worth Noting
Recharge	12	110	Sweetened with grape juice, no sugar added; added sea salt for 50 mg. sodium
Water, tap or bottled		0	No sugar, no fat, no calories, no better choice!

Note that the best fluids for active individuals (you!) are

- Low in caffeine (less than 25 milligrams per serving) or caffeine-free
- Low in sugar (less than 2 teaspoons per serving) or sugar-free
- Low in fat (less than 1 gram per serving) or fat-free
- Moderate in sodium (up to 75 milligrams per serving)
- Naturally rich in vitamins and minerals
- Plain old water

IDEAL EXERCISE LOG

As you know, a helpful tool while making lifestyle changes is your personal journal or daily diary. In the beginning, your log will represent your commitment to change. Put to paper, your exercise goals serve as a plan of action and a promise to yourself that you will PaceWalk regularly and consistently. After a while, you will look to your log as a chance to express yourself as you explore your limits while recognizing your limitations.

A sample log for exercise is given below. You can make photocopies of the sample weekly log or design your own. Bookstores and sporting goods stores sell a variety of exercise calendars that may prove adequate for your needs. You might want to photocopy the phase of the IDEAL Exercise Plan that you are following and keep it with your log. Or you can draw up your own personalized plan for insertion into your log.

FRESH START

I changed my exercise habits before I began to alter my eating habits seriously. I believe that it can prove more effective to begin your lifestyle transformation with exercise. When you become physically active, it may automatically trigger the desire to improve your eating habits. This makes it easier to slowly, gradually, permanently alter your diet. And by exercising regularly, the boost in your body's metabolic rate will speed up the fat loss, so that you can stop dieting and defeat Diet-Induced Overweight once and for all.

SAMPLE LOG

Phase:_____   No. Weeks on Plan:_____   Week's Goal(s):_____

Date	Day of the Week	No. of Minutes of Exercise:		Type of Exercise
		Planned	Performed	
	Monday			
	Tuesday			
	Wednesday			
	Thursday			
	Friday			
	Saturday			
	Sunday			

Total No. of Minutes of Exercise Planned: _____

Total No. of Minutes of Exercise Performed: _____

Comments and Insights:_____

_____

_____

So don't put fitness on hold. If you are ready and willing to get fit and lose fat, improve your health and your self-image, look better and feel better about yourself, *start now!* You will *immediately* feel good, maybe better than you've felt in years. Start now. Go for a walk. *Do it!* After all, you've got nothing to lose—except excess fat!

Go for a walk today, *right now.* Then, when you return feeling refreshed and good about yourself, turn to Section III of this book. It may be the *ideal* time to turn your attention to your eating habits and to learn how you can stop dieting, eat well, and lose that excess body fat—for good.

The IDEAL Eating Plan

7

The IDEAL Eating Plan: Phases I, II, III

When I finally decided to alter my eating habits, I thought I had to give up all my favorite foods, from cheese and cracker snacks to chocolate ice cream desserts, plus red meats and anything else that contained fat. At the time, I was resolute: I didn't want to have a high-fat diet, so I was prepared to make the sacrifice.

However, I quickly discovered that once I eliminated *all* high-fat foods from my diet, there didn't seem to be anything left I liked to eat! So I gave up the idea of giving up all food fat. I decided to approach my eating habits the same way I started exercising: slowly, gradually, comfortably, and at my own pace. I began on the IDEAL Eating Plan (Phase I) and reduced the fat in my diet in easy stages—slowly, gradually, comfortably. And now, several years later, continued adherence to the Phase II/Phase III plan means that I have significantly modified eating habits. And I'm not a bit miserable. In fact, I really *like* my daily diet.

In liberating myself from the burden of perfectionism, it gradually became clear to me that what I really wanted was to be in *reasonably* good physical shape and health. I wanted to lose *some* of my excess fat, enough so that I felt good about myself. I wanted to exercise regularly—often and vigorously enough so that I felt fit. And I wanted to develop dietary patterns that were *low enough* in fat to be healthful but allowed ample room for eating enjoyment.

WHAT DO *YOU* WANT?

Let's be honest: Are you planning to drop down to a body weight that is way below the lowest range you have ever weighed? *Are your goals realistic?*

Complete the self-evaluation that follows in order to set reasonable, attainable personal goals. Record your answers in your IDEAL Log. The more realistic your goals are, the more likely it is that you'll achieve them.

Self-Evaluation: Personal Goals

Part I: Body Image
1. What is a reasonable, realistic weight for you?
2. Have you ever weighed this particular weight? If so, describe the circumstances (your age, lifestyle, how you felt about your body at the time).
3. How long have you been at your current weight?
4. How much time do you expect it will take for you to reach your weight goal? Is this a realistic amount of time?
5. Study yourself in a full-length mirror: Are you fat? Where are your excess fat stores located?
6. Measure the circumference of the widest part of your thighs and upper arms using a tape measure, and record (in inches). How many inches do you need to lose in these spots?
7. Look at your Low-Calorie Overweight Self-Diagnosis from chapter 2. Is your Waist-Hip Ratio too high? If so, how many inches do you need to lose?
8. What size clothing (dress or slacks) do you currently fit into? What is a reasonable, realistic clothing size goal for you?
9. Do other people consider you to be overweight/overfat (that is, has your physician or a loved one suggested that you need to lose weight)?

Part II: Your Eating Habits
1. Is your current diet generally unbalanced?
2. Is your current diet high in fat?
3. Are you restricting your caloric intake? If so, is your current daily intake less than 1200 calories? Less than 1000 calories?
4. Do you usually skip breakfast?
5. Do you often snack or overeat at night?
6. Do you binge eat? How frequently?
7. Do you regularly drink diet soft drinks? Use artificial sweeteners? Buy special "diet" foods?
8. Are you willing to eat more fruits? More vegetables? More breads and cereals? More whole grains? More low-fat dairy products?
9. Are you willing to reduce your intake of high-fat milk products? High-fat meats? High-fat fast foods, snack foods, convenience foods? Fatty foods in general?
10. Are you willing to eat balanced meals? Regular meals? Adequate amounts of low-fat foods—without counting calories, restricting calories, dieting?

Answers to Part I:
Let your answers inform you as to whether your personal weight/body size goals are reasonable, realistic, healthful, doable. You may want to reassess your goals as you progress on this program. That way, if you find that you are not progressing, you can reassess your goals *before* you begin to alter the program—or before you give up on it altogether.

Answers to Part II:
Let your answers inform you as to whether you *need* and *want* to make changes in your current eating practices. Are you willing to give up caloric restrictions, to stop dieting, to eat more food but to eat well, the low-fat way? Let's begin!

EATING THE IDEAL WAY

I've got a surprising and enlightening fact to share with you: Most of us only think we are eating what we like; actually we are eating what we have *learned* to like. Your personal food tastes (and distastes) can be *unlearned* and a new set of eating pleasures discovered to replace the unhealthful old habits.

By incorporating the latest scientific findings in the field of weight control, the IDEAL Eating Plan combines *gradual* change to a low-fat food intake with *tasty* high-nutrient menu choices. You don't eat less, you eat *less fat*. You don't count calories, you *slash fat*. You fend off the starvation response that typically accompanies low-calorie dieting, and you boost your metabolism to shed excess body fat while improving fitness. The IDEAL program will help you to change your tastes and your habits so you can lose weight, overcome Low-Calorie, Diet-Induced Overweight, and get in shape—gradually, enjoyably, permanently.

The IDEAL Eating Plan has been designed to work in three distinct phases. By progressing from Phase I to Phase II and finally to Phase III, you will be able to make dietary changes slowly, comfortably, one step at a time. You'll gradually unlearn old habits. And by personalizing the phases, you will be able to tailor the meals you eat to suit your own needs and tastes.

Before you begin on the IDEAL Eating Plan, read carefully through each of the three phases. Then decide where you want to begin. Most readers will choose to start with Phase I. Unless your diet is already quite low in fat, Phase I will provide ample dietary change for you to start with.

Most people will choose to remain with Phase I for a minimum of four to six weeks. You will lose weight and fat on the IDEAL Eating Plan in Phase I, and then for as long as you follow Phase II. Be aware that Phase II is lower in fat than Phase I, yet the calories are relatively the same. Fat reduction, *not calorie-cutting*, is the key to safe, effective, permanent weight loss!

You can remain on Phase II until you have reached your IDEAL weight/fat-loss goal. Phase III is even lower in fat, but you can *eat more* to offset further weight loss, if so desired. This is the *lifelong* maintenance phase.

Note that *you may not be cutting calories on the IDEAL Eating Plan, but you will be shedding unwanted fat*—from your diet *and* from your body.

SOME DEFINITIONS

In each phase of the IDEAL Eating Plan, you will customize your diet using the following:

- Primary foods
- Complementary foods
- The Fat Counter (see chapter 9)
- Fat slashing tips
- Ideal meal choices
- Tips for IDEAL nutrition

The *primary foods* form the foundation of your diet, with a variety of *complementary foods* for fun and flavor. By using the Fat Counter (a detailed chart given in the next chapter, indicating the teaspoons of fat in everyday foods) and the fat slashing tips, you can control the amount of fat you include in making your daily meal choices for breakfast, lunch, dinner, and snacks—at each phase of the IDEAL plan. The tips for IDEAL nutrition given with each phase help you to improve the quality of your meals gradually as you reduce the dietary fat—and your body fat! Just about everything you need to embark on a new way of eating—gradually, sensibly, enjoyably—is included in each phase of the IDEAL Eating Plan.

Be sure to set reasonable goals at each phase—don't try to make all the changes, slash all the fat, achieve all the nutrition goals all at once. Let yourself adjust to each change you make before making more. Go slowly, and take it easy.

Remember, the IDEAL Weight-Loss Program is not like fad diets, which tell you exactly what to eat and when to eat it. On this program, it is up to you to make the best choices, to make the food (and exercise) decisions best for you. You design your own menus and create or revise your own recipes. For assistance, you can refer to the guidelines provided in chapters 9 and 10.

It is a good idea to *begin eating on a regular schedule.* Irregular meals and meal skipping encourage fat storage and slow metabolism to thwart weight-loss efforts. Breakfast is very important, so don't skip it! And don't skimp on lunch, because if you do, it is a good bet that you'll then make up for your restrictive eating by overeating during the evening hours.

Note that the IDEAL meal choices are divided into five categories—three regular meals, plus fast food options and snacks. You can refer to the recommended number of daily servings and serving size when making your menu choices, and use your Fat Counter (see chapter 9) to keep your fat intake within the recommended guidelines per meal or snack. But remember, the meal choices given are only suggestions. Use your own imagination! With this eating plan, it is up to *you* to choose the low-fat foods you want to eat.

In each phase, everything is laid out for you, step by step. So, relax! All you have to do is *take the first step.* You'll soon find that you enjoy it, and you'll feel better about your eating patterns and yourself.

YOUR FAT GOALS

The typical American female consumes over 100 grams, or 20 teaspoons, of fat a day, which is equivalent to more than 900 calories. The average American male consumes over 125 grams, or 25 teaspoons, of fat in his daily diet, accounting for some 1125 calories. (To give you a sense of how much that is, note that a stick of butter is equivalent to 24 teaspoons of fat.)

So what would be an ideal fat intake? Check the figures in the two charts that follow. Your current fat intake is probably similar to most Americans'. As you progress from phase to phase on this program, substituting new fat goals for old fat intake habits, you will achieve your fat reduction goals—in your diet *and* your body.

IDEAL FOOD, IDEAL NUTRITION

At each phase of the IDEAL Eating Plan, your food intake will provide you with optimal nutrition and ample energy but *less fat.* You will be eating more food. You will receive an abundance of nutrients, but you will be minimizing your fat intake. Because the eating plans given are well balanced and do not cut calories to the

AVERAGE AMERICAN DIET
Over 40% Fat

Total Calories per Day	Fat in Grams	Fat in Teaspoons
1200	> 55	11+
1500	> 70	14+
2000	> 90	18+
2500	>115	23+
3000	>135	27+

IDEAL DIET
Under 30% Fat

Total Calories per Day	Fat in Grams	Fat in Teaspoons
1500*	< 50	< 10
1800	< 60	< 12
2000	< 65	< 13
2400	< 80	< 16
3000	<100	< 20

*Note that the IDEAL diet includes 1500 calories per day or more. Low-calorie diets encourage Low-Calorie Overweight so are not considered productive or healthy.

bone, you won't need to turn to nutritional supplementation or rely on diet foods (more on this later).

The IDEAL Eating Plan provides this ideal combination of foods and nutrients at each phase:

- Carbohydrates (complex starches and natural sugars)—55 to 60 percent of daily calories
- Protein (animal and vegetable)—10 to 15 percent of daily calories
- Fat—30 percent or less of daily calories

As you slowly progress from Phase I to Phase II and finally move on to Phase III, the percentage of fat in your diet will gradually decrease. Protein, too, will decrease in proportion. Carbohydrate will continue to provide the greatest percentage of daily nutrition and energy.

On each phase of the IDEAL program, energy-rich carbohydrates and lean proteins will serve as your *primary foods,* to be consumed in low-fat food packages. In reducing your fat intake, animal protein foods like red meats and poultry will become *complementary foods* instead of primary food choices. Thus, the foods you will be eating at each phase can be categorized in these two groups:

- *Primary foods*—supply most of your daily calories; include *complex carbohydrates* (such as breads, cereals, pasta, rice, potatoes, dried beans and peas), foods rich in *natural sugars* (such as fruits and vegetables), and *lean protein* sources (such as low-fat milk and cheese, fish and other seafood)
- *Complementary foods*—may provide some protein but also add to *fat* intakes (such foods include red meats, peanut butter, and nuts), simply furnish energy as fat (as do vegetable oils and margarine), or are low in nutrient value but high in calories (notably, sweets and alcoholic beverages)

THE IDEAL EATING PLAN—PHASE I

In this phase, the typical 42 percent fat diet, which contains 65 to 88 grams of fat (13 to 18 teaspoons of fat) will be reduced gradually to the Phase II fat goal of 30 percent—that is, 50 to 65 grams of fat (10 to 13 teaspoons of fat) per day.

Remember to start slowly and to progress gradually. Don't try to make all of the changes at once. Make them one at a time, and let your body and your taste buds adjust.

SERVING SIZES/FOOD EQUIVALENTS

Meat, poultry, seafood:

4 ounces raw meat = 3 ounces trimmed, cooked meat

3 ounces meat or poultry = a piece the size of a deck of cards

3 ounces fish = ½ cup canned or one piece measuring 3 × 2½ × ½ inches fresh

3 ounces shellfish = 10 oysters, 10 scallops, 12 shrimp, or 12 clams

Fats: The following all contain 1 teaspoon of fat:

1 teaspoon butter or margarine (stick, soft, or squeeze)

1 teaspoon vegetable oil, salad dressing, or mayonnaise

2 teaspoons chopped nuts, seeds, or peanut butter

1 tablespoon low-calorie salad dressing or sliced olives

⅛ avocado or 10 small olives

Sweets:

1 serving = the amount providing 2 to 3 teaspoons of fat (as allowed for snacks). Use your Fat Counter (see chapter 8) to help you determine serving sizes.

Alcohol: 1 serving equals:

12 ounces light beer (average can)

3½ ounces dry wine (average wineglass)

1½ ounces "hard" liquor (average shot of vodka, gin, whiskey, etc.)

Fish
$3 \times 4 \times \frac{3}{4}$ inches =
3 ounces

This thick

Chicken Leg and Thigh
This size =
3 ounces

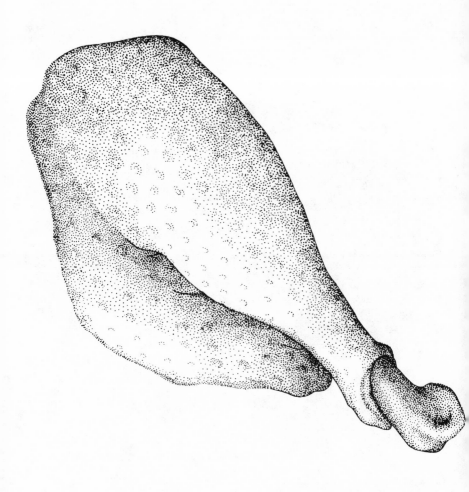

Illustrations by Jackie Aher

Roast Turkey
Two slices this size =
3 ounces

This thick

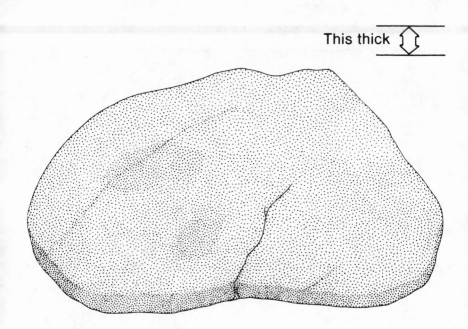

Hamburger (Lean)
One patty this size =
3 ounces

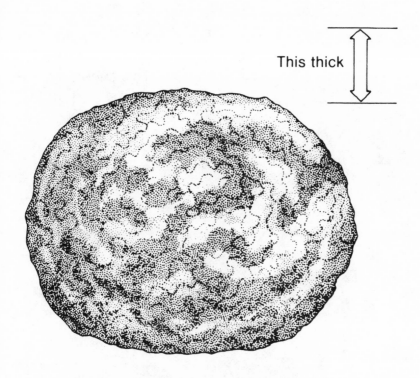

This thick

Lamb Chop
Two chops this size =
3 ounces

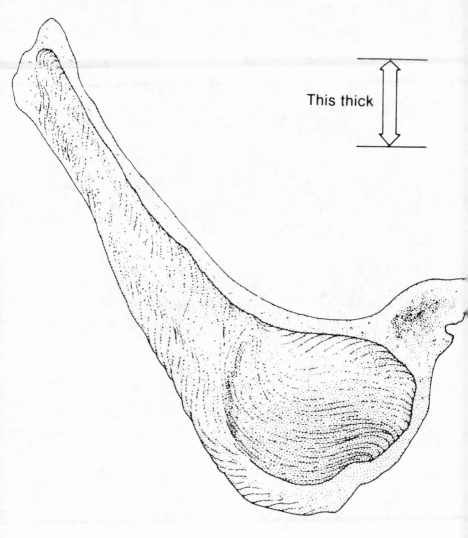

This thick

Pork Chop (Lean Only)
Two chops this size =
(fat removed)
3 ounces

This thick

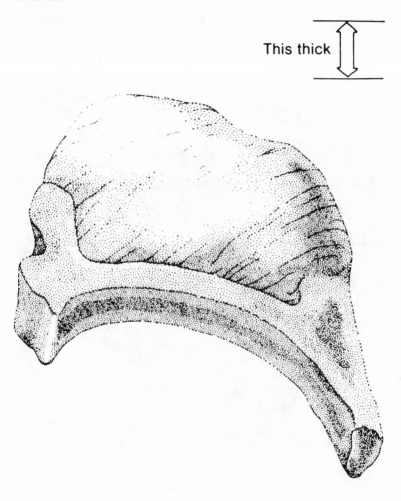

Beef Steak
$3 \times 3 \times 3/4$ inches =
3 ounces

This thick

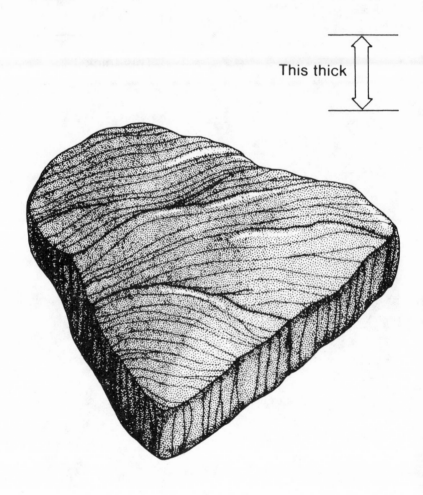

Roast Beef (Lean Only)
Two slices this size =
3 ounces

This thick

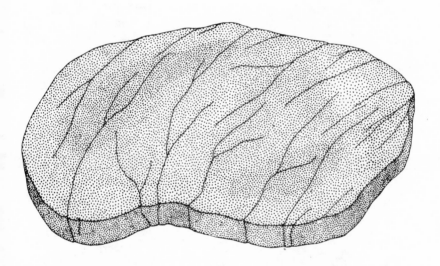

PRIMARY FOODS

You should eat a variety of foods every day from each of the indicated basic food groups and in the recommended numbers of daily servings and serving sizes.

BASIC FOOD GROUP	NO. SERVINGS DAILY	SERVING SIZE
Fruits and vegetables	5–7	1 whole fruit ½ cup juice 1 cup raw fruit or vegetable ½ cup cooked fruit or vegetable
Breads and cereals	5–7	1 slice bread 1 small roll, pita, muffin, pancake, waffle, tortilla ½ bagel, English muffin ½–¾ cup cereal or cooked whole grain ½ cup plain pasta ¾ cup cooked rice 1½ cups air-popped popcorn
Milk and cheese	3–4	1 cup skim or low-fat milk or yogurt 1½ oz. low- or medium-fat cheese 4 Tbsp. grated Parmesan cheese
Meat alternates	2 (but keep to 3 egg yolks or less per week; have 6–7 oz. fish or shellfish a week)	1 egg 3 oz. fish ½ cup cottage cheese ½ cup dried beans or peas

Grains and dried beans or peas that are appropriate choices as meat alternates include the following:

- Grains: cornmeal, grits, barley, bulgur, buckwheat, kasha, millet, rye berries, wheat berries, soy grits
- Dried beans: aduki, black, fava, garbanzo, great northern, kidney, lima, mung, navy, pea, pinto, soy (tofu)
- Dried peas: black-eyed, chick, cow, field, split
- Lentils

COMPLEMENTARY FOODS

Keep intake of these foods down to minimize your daily intake of fat:

FOOD GROUP	DAILY INTAKE LIMIT
Meat and poultry	6–7 oz. maximum
Fats	4–5 tsp. maximum (as added fat)
Sweets and alcohol	up to 2 servings each maximum (if desired)

IDEAL MEAL CHOICES

You can obtain your *daily servings* from the basic food groups by selecting your meals and snacks from the foods in the lists that follow. Be sure to adhere to the given limits on teaspoons of fat per meal by using your Fat Counter to guide your serving sizes.

BREAKFAST
(3–4 teaspoons of fat)

Fresh fruit
Fruit juice
Canned fruit in juice or light syrup
Fortified ready-to-eat cold cereal with 2% low-fat milk
Oatmeal or other hot cereal with 2% low-fat milk
Grits
Bagel
English muffin
Toast
Bran, corn, or fruit muffin
Pancake with syrup
Waffle with syrup
Coffee or tea with 2% low-fat milk (if desired)
Low-fat yogurt (on cereal or fruit)

LUNCH
(4–5 teaspoons of fat)

Vegetable juice
Gazpacho
Vegetable soup
Fresh fruit salad with cottage cheese
Salads with medium-fat cheese and low-calorie dressing
French bread
Italian bread
Enriched bread or rolls
Pita bread
Rice cakes
Matzoh, melba toast
Breadsticks
Cornbread
Tuna, salmon, or mackerel (fresh or canned in water)
Frozen vegetable-topped pizza (1 serving)
Fast food options (see below)

DINNER
(4–5 teaspoons of fat)

Lean red meats
Wild game
Poultry (skinless)
Barbecued chicken (skinless)
Salmon or herring
Shellfish
Plain pasta—spaghetti, macaroni, noodles—with meatless tomato
    sauce
Vegetable pasta with meatless tomato sauce
Chop suey
Chow mein
Vegetable stir-fry with lean meats
"Lite" frozen meals
Vegetable-topped pizza
Saffron rice, rice pilaf
Baked potato, sweet potato
Corn on the cob
Steamed vegetables

FAST FOOD OPTIONS
($<$4 teaspoons of fat)

Beef burrito
Roast beef sandwich
Cheeseburger
Hamburger
Taco
Bean burrito
Bean tostada
Cheese pizza
Baked potato (plain)
Salad bar (low-fat choices only)

SNACKS
(2–3 teaspoons of fat)

Ice milk
Sherbet
Low-fat yogurt (fruited or flavored, if desired)
Sponge cake
Angel food cake
Fig bars
Gingersnaps
Oatmeal cookies
Animal crackers
Graham crackers
Popcorn (air-popped)
Pretzels
Low-fat crackers with medium-fat cheese

FAT SLASHING

Slowly but steadily, make the following food substitutions to gradually lower your fat intake.

- Substitute 2 percent low-fat milk and yogurt for whole milk.
- Substitute 2 percent low-fat milk for cream.
- Substitute sherbet, ice milk, or frozen low-fat yogurt for ice cream.
- Substitute medium-fat cheeses for high-fat cheeses (see chart on pages 185–187).
- Substitute well-trimmed, select cuts of red meat for marbled prime or choice cuts.
- Remove skin from poultry before cooking.
- Substitute reduced amounts of soft or squeeze margarine for butter and stick margarine.
- Reduce intake of high-fat foods (see lists on pages 140–141).

FOR IDEAL NUTRITION

One at a time, incorporate the following steps to optimal nutrition into your eating plan:

- Eat fruits and vegetables plain, raw, or lightly steamed.
- Substitute fruits canned in juice or light syrup for heavy syrup–packed canned fruits.
- Choose enriched breads, pastas, or other grain products.
- Choose fortified cereals.
- Limit high-fat meats that are also high in sodium (e.g., bacon, cold cuts, hot dogs, sausage; see list on pages 146–147).
- Limit egg yolks to two or three per week.
- Limit organ meats to once a month.
- Limit high-cholesterol foods (see list on pages 141–142).
- Alter recipes to reduce cholesterol.
- Alter recipes to reduce fat.
- Select new recipes that are low in fat and cholesterol.

IDEAL EATING PLAN—PHASE II

In this phase, you will reach and maintain the fat goal of 30 percent fat—that is, 50 to 65 grams of fat (10 to 13 teaspoons of fat) per day.

Remember to go slowly and to make changes one at a time. You have plenty of time to improve your eating habits, so don't rush it and don't push it.

PRIMARY FOODS

You should eat a variety of foods every day from each of the indicated basic food groups and in the recommended number of daily servings and serving sizes.

BASIC FOOD GROUP	NO. SERVINGS DAILY	SERVING SIZE
Fruits and vegetables	6–7	1 whole fruit ½ cup juice 1 cup raw fruit or vegetable ½ cup cooked fruit or vegetable

BASIC FOOD GROUP	NO. SERVINGS DAILY	SERVING SIZE
Breads and cereals*	6–7	1 slice bread 1 small roll, pita, muffin, pancake, waffle, tortilla ½ bagel, English muffin ½–¾ cup cereal or cooked whole grain ½ cup plain pasta ¾ cup cooked rice 1½ cups air-popped popcorn
Milk and cheese	3–4 (low-fat only)	1 cup skim or low-fat milk or yogurt 1½ oz. low-fat cheese 4 Tbsp. grated Parmesan cheese
Meat alternates*	2 (but keep to 2–3 egg yolks or less per week; have 12–14 oz. fish or shellfish a week; have meatless meals at least 3 times a week)	1 egg 3 oz. fish ½ cup low-fat cottage cheese ½ cup dried beans or peas

*For choices of grains and dried beans or peas, see the list given after the primary foods chart for Phase I.

COMPLEMENTARY FOODS

Keep intake of these foods down to minimize your daily intake of fat:

FOOD GROUP	DAILY INTAKE LIMIT
Meat and poultry	5–6 oz. maximum
Fats	3–4 tsp. maximum (as added fat)

FOOD GROUP	DAILY INTAKE LIMIT
Sweets and alcohol	Up to 1 serving each maximum (if desired)

IDEAL MEAL CHOICES

You can obtain your *daily servings* from the basic food groups by selecting your meals and snacks from the foods in the lists that follow. Be sure to adhere to the given limits on teaspoons of fat per meal by using your Fat Counter to guide your serving sizes.

BREAKFAST
(2–3 teaspoons of fat)

Fresh fruit
Fruit juice
Canned fruit in juice or light syrup
Whole-grain ready-to-eat cereal with 1% low-fat milk
Whole-grain hot cereals (oatmeal, Wheatena) with 1% low-fat milk
Grits
Whole-grain bagels
Whole-wheat English muffins
Whole-grain toast
Homemade low-fat whole-grain or buckwheat pancakes with syrup
Homemade low-fat whole-grain waffles with syrup
Low-fat yogurt (on cereal or fruit)
Hot cocoa

LUNCH
(3 teaspoons of fat)

Lentil soup
Bean soup
Homemade vegetable soup
Low-sodium canned vegetable soup
Fresh artichoke with lemon juice
Raw vegetable crudités
Salads with low-fat cheese and vinegar and lemon juice

Fresh fruit salad with low-fat cottage cheese or yogurt (if desired)
Whole-grain bread or rolls
Whole-wheat pita bread
Whole-grain low-fat crackers (unsalted)
Whole-grain unsalted matzoh or melba toast
Whole-grain unsalted breadsticks
Brown rice cakes or crackers (unsalted)
Tuna, salmon, or mackerel (fresh or canned in water)
Fast food options (see below)

DINNER
(3–4 teaspoons of fat)

Lean meat or poultry as condiments
Vegetable stir-fry with tofu
Clams, mussels, or oysters
White fish (baked or broiled)
Soy noodles
Whole-grain pastas with clam, marinara, or tomato sauce
Vegetable-topped pizza
Homemade chop suey, chow mein
Vegetarian baked beans
Meatless chili
Black beans and rice
Red beans and rice
Brown rice or wild rice
Kasha, millet, or polenta
Homemade whole-grain stuffing
Baked potato with low-fat yogurt or mock sour cream (see recipe, page 188)
Baked sweet potato or yams
Plantain or parsnips (baked)
Corn on the cob
Steamed vegetables

FAST FOOD OPTIONS
(<2 teaspoons of fat)

Bean burrito
Bean tostada
Cheese pizza
Baked potato (plain)
Salad bar (low-fat, low-sodium choices only)

SNACKS
(2–3 teaspoons of fat)

Hummus with whole-wheat pita bread
Unsalted whole-wheat pretzels
Unsalted whole-grain crackers with low-fat cheese
Angel food cake with puréed strawberries
Poached fruit in light syrup
Fruit sorbet
Frozen fruit bars

FAT SLASHING

Gradually reduce your fat intake by incorporating the following food substitutions—slowly, steadily, one at a time.

- Substitute 1 percent low-fat milk for 2 percent low-fat milk.
- Substitute low-fat cheeses for medium- and high-fat cheeses (see chart on pages 185–187).
- Substitute fruit sorbets and fruit ices for sherbet and ice milk.
- Substitute low-fat homemade baked goods for commercial baked goods.
- Substitute low-fat yogurt or mock sour cream (see recipe on page 188) for sour cream.
- Substitute vegetable oil for shortening, lard, or animal fats in cooking.
- Substitute cocoa powder for chocolate in cooking or baking.
- Limit high-fat foods (see lists on pages 140–141).

FOR IDEAL NUTRITION

You can *slowly* enhance the overall nutritional value of your eating plan by making the following dietary alterations—one at a time.

- Substitute puréed fruits for whipped topping.
- Substitute puréed vegetables for flour and fat to thicken sauces.
- Eat fruits and vegetables whole, with skins and seeds.
- Substitute whole-grain breads and cereals and other whole-grain products for those made with enriched grains.
- Substitute cereals with 3 to 4 grams of fiber or more per serving for other ready-to-eat cereals (see list below).
- Introduce more recipes using dried beans and peas, other starchy vegetable dishes
- Substitute natural peanut butter for commercial, hydrogenated brands.
- Limit salt in cooking and at the table.
- Limit foods high in sodium (see page 169).
- Limit caffeinated beverages to four per day.
- Alter recipes to reduce salt.
- Alter recipes to increase fiber.
- Select new recipes that are low in fat and sodium, high in fiber.

FIBER-RICH CEREAL CHOICES

Cereals with 3–4 Grams Fiber per Serving	Cereals with Over 4 Grams Fiber per Serving
Oats, oatmeal	All Bran
40% Bran Flakes	Bran Buds
Cracklin' Bran	Bran Chex
Raisin Bran	Corn Bran
Grape Nuts	Oat Bran
Most	
Shredded Wheat	

THE IDEAL EATING PLAN—PHASE III

In this phase, you will gradually drop your total fat intake below 30 percent—that is, to less than 50 to 65 grams of fat (less than 10 to 13 teaspoons of fat) per day. But don't forgo your eating pleasure by attempting to reduce fat intake to an unpalatable amount! Don't overdo, just be moderate. For *weight loss,* include the suggested daily servings outlined below. As a *maintenance plan,* adjust food intake to prevent further weight loss by increasing daily servings and portion sizes of the primary foods.

PRIMARY FOODS

You should eat a variety of foods every day from each of the indicated basic food groups and in the recommended number of daily servings and serving sizes.

BASIC FOOD GROUP	NO. SERVINGS DAILY	SERVING SIZE
Fruits and vegetables	6–7	1 whole fruit ½ cup juice 1 cup raw fruit or vegetable ½ cup cooked fruit or vegetable
Breads and cereals*	6–7	1 slice bread 1 small roll, pita, muffin, pancake, waffle, tortilla ½ bagel, English muffin ½–¾ cup cereal or cooked whole grain ½ cup plain pasta ¾ cup cooked rice 1½ cups air-popped popcorn

*For choices of grains and dried beans or peas, see the list given after the primary foods chart for Phase I.

BASIC FOOD GROUP	NO. SERVINGS DAILY	SERVING SIZE
Milk and cheese	3–4 (low-fat only)	1 cup skim or low-fat milk or yogurt 1½ oz. low-fat cheese 4 Tbsp. grated Parmesan cheese
Meat alternates*	2 (but keep to 1–2 egg yolks or less per week; have 18–20 oz. fish or shellfish per week; have meatless meals at least 5 times a week)	1 egg 3 oz. fish ½ cup low-fat cottage cheese ½ cup dried beans or peas

COMPLEMENTARY FOODS

Keep intake of these foods down to minimize your daily intake of fat:

FOOD GROUP	DAILY INTAKE LIMIT
Meat and poultry	3–5 oz. maximum
Fats	No more than 3 tsp. (as added fat)
Sweets	Limit to special occasions (if desired); limit to choices with less than 2 tsp. fat
Alcohol	No more than 1 serving daily (if any)

IDEAL MEAL CHOICES

You can obtain your *daily servings* from the basic food groups by selecting your meals and snacks from the foods in the lists that follow. Be sure to adhere to the given limits on teaspoons of fat per meal by using your Fat Counter to guide your serving sizes.

BREAKFAST
(2 teaspoons of fat)

Fresh fruit
Fruit juice
Juice-packed canned fruit
Whole-grain ready-to-eat cereal with skim milk
Whole-grain hot cereals, oatmeal, or oat bran with skim milk
Whole-grain bagels
Whole-wheat English muffins with all-fruit preserves (if desired)
Whole-grain toast with all-fruit preserves (if desired)
Nonfat yogurt (on cereal or fruit)
Decaffeinated coffee or herb tea

LUNCH
(3 teaspoons of fat)

Vegetable or bean soup (homemade)
Fresh artichoke with lemon juice
Raw vegetable crudités
Salads with vinegar and lemon juice as dressing
Fresh fruit salad with low-fat cottage cheese or yogurt (if desired)
Whole-grain bread or rolls
Whole-grain pita bread
Crispbread or rye crisp (unsalted)
Whole-wheat matzoh or unsalted melba toast (unsalted)
Whole-grain breadsticks (unsalted)
Brown rice cakes or crackers (unsalted)
Tuna, salmon, or mackerel (fresh or canned in water)
Fast food options (see below)

DINNER
(3 teaspoons of fat)

Vegetable stir-fry
Whole-grain pastas with clam, marinara, or tomato sauce
Soy noodles
Homemade meatless chop suey or chow mein
Homemade low-fat vegetable pizza

Vegetarian baked beans
Meatless chili
Beans and rice
Brown rice or wild rice
Kasha, millet, or polenta
Baked potato with low-fat yogurt or mock sour cream (see page 188)
Baked sweet potato or yams
Baked parsnips or plantains
Corn on the cob
Steamed vegetables

FAST FOOD OPTIONS
(<2 teaspoons of fat)

Bean burrito
Bean tostada
Cheese pizza
Baked potato (plain)
Salad bar (low-fat, low-sodium, unsweetened choices only)

SNACKS
(<2 teaspoons of fat)

Fresh fruit
Juice-packed canned fruit
Applesauce
Dried fruits
Baked apple with cinnamon and raisins
Crudités
Unsalted whole-wheat pretzels
Unsalted whole-grain fat-free crackers
Air-popped popcorn

FAT SLASHING

You can gradually reduce your daily fat intake by making the following food substitutions—one at a time.

- Substitute applesauce or all-fruit preserves for soft margarine.
- Substitute lemon juice for soft margarine on vegetables.

- Substitute skim milk for 1 percent low-fat milk.
- Substitute fat-free salad dressings for low-calorie dressings.
- Limit high-fat foods to special occasions (see lists on pages 140–141).

FOR IDEAL NUTRITION

You can maximize your nutritional intakes by making the following dietary alterations—one at a time.

- Substitute juices and water for soft drinks or diet soft drinks.
- Reduce sugar used in cooking and at the table.
- Limit foods high in sugar (see list on pages 145–146).
- Limit caffeinated beverages to two per day or less.
- Alter recipes to reduce sugar.
- Select new recipes that are sugar-free and very low in fat or fat-free.

WHAT ABOUT DIET FOODS?

Americans spend over $20 billion annually on diet foods and beverages. Yet for most waist watchers, the only thing lost is the money used to buy such products.

Studies have shown that people who drink diet soft drinks are *not* more successful at losing weight than those who shun artificially sweetened beverages. In fact, some researchers believe that the use of aspartame, saccharin, and other superconcentrated sweeteners stimulates the desire for sweet foods and causes people to eat more, usually in the form of sugar-rich *and high-fat* desserts. A study conducted by the American Cancer Society found that long-term users of artificial sweeteners were more apt to *gain* weight, primarily because they didn't utilize the diet substances as food substitutes but used them in addition to their normal food intakes. It is the *fat* calories, not the sugar calories (simple carbohydrates) that are of primary concern for those of us trying to control our weight.

What about the new fake fats? Will these prove to be the weight-loss magic many dieters are hoping for? Personally, I am reserving judgment. Olestra, the "sucrose polyester" fat replacement, is noncaloric and would be used as a cooking oil substitute in snack foods. However, safety concerns have delayed marketing. For one thing, Olestra appears to reduce vitamin absorption. NutraSweet's fake fat "Simplesse" is made with processed proteins, so it is not *calorie*-free. Simplesse is, however, a fat-free fat substitute and has been proposed for use in uncooked foods to replace traditional ice cream, salad dressings, mayonnaise, butter, cheese spreads, and cream cheese.

Even if either of these products is ever approved as safe, it is unlikely that dieters who eat foods containing the fake fats will lose weight *unless they exercise regularly and follow a low-fat eating plan* as well.

ON THE RIGHT TRACK

Your IDEAL Log will serve as an essential tool for recording both your food intake and your personal feelings as you begin on and adjust to each phase of the IDEAL Eating Plan. When you embark on each phase, carefully record your food intake every day to be sure that you are on track. And try to jot down how you are feeling—your frustrations, discoveries, ideas, fears—to provide insight into your emotional and physical reactions to your changes in eating practices. If you find that you are overly stressed by the phase you have selected, switch to a more liberal phase until you are ready to move on. And when on a weight maintenance plan, you can record your food intake while you adjust portions and servings until your weight is stabilized as desired.

, Since you will want to make dietary changes in a gradual manner, you may remain at one phase for a period of several weeks or even months. The frequency of dietary record keeping during this time is up to you. Personally, I find it very helpful to keep a daily record of my exercise patterns, but I only record my dietary intake during those times when I am stressed or in the midst of making a significant change. For example, if I notice that my clothes feel tight, I might check my log to see if my dietary habits are at fault. Or if I have decided to alter my eating patterns (for example, eating more fish during a vacation by the sea), I try to record the week's intake in my log.

The Healthy Weight goal you recorded in your IDEAL Log can also be a helpful tool for keeping you on track—as long as you only weigh yourself once a week *at the most,* that is. To avoid the disillusionment that accompanies reliance on scale weight as an indicator of success, I would suggest that you *wait to weigh in until four weeks after you adopt the IDEAL Eating Plan.*

If you prefer, Phase II can serve as a more liberal maintenance plan than Phase III once you have achieved your weight-loss goals. Be sure to increase servings of fruits, vegetables, and grain products if your weight continues to drop. On your maintenance plan, you can also "cheat" by indulging in food favorites every now and then, although it is likely that your changing tastes will alter your choices for the kind, frequency, and quantity of special treats. That has certainly happened to me. Although I still like the tastes, my body's tolerance for chocolate, ice cream, and cheese has dropped sharply.

The next chapter will help you to *stay* on the IDEAL Eating Plan—at home, in the supermarket, in your favorite restaurants, and wherever else you may be while you're losing weight and keeping it off.

8

The IDEAL Diet—
Without Dieting!

I used to eat chocolate candy bars several times a week. I frequently ate the richest, creamiest chocolate ice cream available. In between, I rivaled the Cookie Monster, munching away on packages of my favorite brands of cookies (mostly chocolate, of course). I also loved fatty meats. Bacon was on my breakfast menu quite regularly, and beef was on my dinner plate four or five nights a week. Cheese was another one of my favorites; I could consume one to two pounds of it a week (the equivalent of consuming three to six *cups* of fat)! And yet I considered my diet to be a healthy one.

As you know, I have altered my diet dramatically. But I don't feel depressed, deprived, or like a diet martyr, because *my tastes have changed.* Gradually, as I ate less of my former favorites, I craved them less. Now if I eat too much fat, I get an unpleasant overfull feeling in my throat that tells me loud and clear that I overdid it.

WHAT WORKS FOR YOU

What worked for me can also work for you. The key is to *individualize a step-by-step plan* for reducing the fat in your current diet, allowing yourself to adjust to your new way of eating until it becomes second nature. Don't rush it—you won't be able to alter your eating patterns in a day or a week. But you can personalize a plan that suits your tastes, your needs, your lifestyle. And you can adopt it *gradually,* so that your palate and your psyche have time to get used to a new way of eating.

By following the three phases of graduated reduced-fat eating, you won't starve, you won't need to count calories, you won't "diet." But you *will* lose weight. And you *will* feel healthier. But you have to begin; you must *do it!*

Remember how long it took me to start exercising after I first realized that I needed to start, that I wanted to start, that I *had* to start? Well, it also took me a while to change my diet once I realized that I needed, wanted, *had* to eat better. I thought about my waistline for years, watching it expand while I snacked on yet another box of chocolate chip cookies. When I finally began jogging, then racing, I began to think about eating better for improved performance. But I didn't actually do anything about it for a long time.

TIME FOR TRANSITION

In 1978, I designed a nutrition course for the School of Medicine at the State University of New York at Stony Brook, where I teach. Like most medical schools, there was no required course in nutrition (and there still isn't). Since I did not have the opportunity to take any nutrition courses during my own medical training, the course-designing effort served as my first in-depth exposure to the field.

When I planned *Triathloning for Ordinary Mortals*, I knew that I needed to include a chapter on eating for endurance, but I felt hesitant about my suitability as a nutrition expert. So I enlisted the aid of registered dietitian Virginia Aronson, my coauthor on this book and a nutritionist at Harvard University at the time. She showed me how best to fuel my body for athletic training—and how to eat the low-fat way. As soon as I read Virginia's nutrition chapter for my triathlon book, I realized that it was indeed time to change my diet. And when I decided to write this book, I asked Virginia to advise me on the IDEAL Eating Plan.

Interestingly enough, Virginia's typing service was so inspired by the IDEAL Eating Plan that several of the women adopted the program themselves. As this goes to press, Beth has shed twenty pounds, Mary bicycles and PaceWalks daily, and both have abandoned futile, low-calorie diets for eating healthfully the low-fat nutrition way.

FIRST, SELF-EVALUATE

"I'm already an expert in nutrition," you say. "I know all about healthy foods, nutrient values, and calories, calories, calories!" That's great! But are you up on all of the latest discoveries in the field? Do you know that obsessive calorie-counting can really hurt you? (I never do it.) That it's the high fat content in foods that really hurts, as Surgeon General C. Everett Koop stated in 1988? That fat-lowering is the most healthy thing you can do for yourself both for weight and fat loss and protection against heart disease?

Take a close look at your nutrition know-how with the self-evaluation that follows. You can record your answers in your IDEAL Log for future reference.

Self-Evaluation: Nutrition Know-How

1. List your ten all-time favorite foods and describe how often you usually eat/drink them (on the hour every hour, daily, once a week, once a year, etc.).
2. Are your food favorites:

   High in fat?   High in Protein?
   High in cholesterol?   High in starch?
   High in sugar?   High in fiber?
   High in sodium (salt)?   Vitamin-rich?
   Alcoholic?   Mineral-rich?

3. Do you eat at least two servings of fruit daily?
4. Do you eat at least two servings of vegetables daily?
5. Do you usually choose whole-grain breads and cereals?
6. Do you drink low-fat or skim milk daily? Eat low-fat cheeses? Eat low-fat yogurt?

7. Do you limit your red meat intake to less than five times per week?
8. Do you remove the skin from poultry before eating or cooking?
9. Do you eat fish several times a week?
10. Do you include dried beans and peas at least several times a week?
11. Do you limit your egg intake to three yolks or less per week?
12. Do you usually have a meatless lunch?
13. Do you usually have a meatless dinner?
14. Do you use cream or half-and-half in coffee or tea?
15. Do you add butter or margarine to vegetables, breads, other foods?
16. Do you eat fried foods?
17. Do you have a "sweet tooth"? (C'mon, admit it!)
18. Do you use table sugar or honey in coffee and tea? On cereal? On fruit?
19. Do you usually eat dessert after lunch? After dinner?
20. Do you drink soft drinks? Diet soft drinks?
21. Do you like—and eat—salty foods?
22. Do you usually add salt to your food at the table or in cooking?
23. Do you frequently eat salted snack foods such as chips and pretzels?
24. Do you frequently eat at fast food restaurants?
25. Do you drink alcoholic beverages daily—more than two drinks a day?

Answers to Self-Evaluation:

1–2.   If you favor high-fat, sweet, and rich foodstuffs and indulge in them often, your diet is probably not ideal. If you prefer more nutritious foods, you may already be on your way to eating the ideal way.

3–13.   The more "yes" answers, the more likely your diet is ideal.

14–25.   The more "no" answers, the more likely your diet is ideal.

So, are you already eating an ideally balanced diet? Or are you thinking about eating a balanced diet but actually eating in a way that is less than ideal? If you adopt the IDEAL Eating Plan, you'll be eating a balanced diet and getting all of the nutrients you need for good health *while you're losing weight.*

IDEAL DIETARY GUIDELINES

The nutritional basis for the IDEAL Eating Plan is the federal government's "Dietary Guidelines for Americans." These guidelines were reviewed in the 1988 U.S. Surgeon General's nutrition report and are still considered by nutrition experts to be the best dietary advice available:

- Eat a variety of foods.
- Maintain a desirable (i.e., healthy) weight.
- Avoid too much fat, saturated fat, and cholesterol.
- Eat foods with adequate starch and fiber.
- Avoid too much sugar.
- Avoid too much sodium.
- If you drink alcoholic beverages, do so in moderation.

These guidelines are designed for healthy Americans who do not need special diets due to illness or conditions that interfere with nutritional requirements. This is also true for the IDEAL Eating Plan. If you need a special diet as prescribed by your physician, you should seek individualized instructions from a registered dietitian (R.D.) or other nutrition professional. But if you are in generally good health and simply want to shed some fat and/ or eat a more balanced diet, following the Dietary Guidelines by adopting the IDEAL Eating Plan can help you do so.

VARIETY AND MODERATION

Since you need to obtain more than forty nutrients from your food (proteins, carbohydrates, essential fats, vitamins, and minerals in amounts dependent on your age, sex, size, and health), and since no single food contains all of these essential factors in adequate amounts, eating a *varied* diet is important. Low-calorie diets can short-change you of essential nutrients. The IDEAL Eating Plan provides all the nutrients you need for good health. Plus, if you eat an ideal *varied* diet, you won't need to rely on vitamin supplements. Practice moderation in food portions, and you can enjoy a *wide* variety of foods—while you shed extra pounds.

The third Dietary Guideline, however, is really the main focal point of the IDEAL Eating Plan: reducing dietary fat. All fats are alike in that they are *all* heavyweights when it comes to their caloric contributions. However, the *type* of fat you select *does* make a difference in the overall effects on health. Diets high in *saturated* fats appear to be associated with chronic disease, notably heart disease. Diets that emphasize *unsaturated* fats instead seem to reduce the risks for serious illness, as long as the diet is not high in *total* fat content. The desirable balance is a low-fat diet, with most of the fat in unsaturated forms:

- *Polyunsaturated* fats are abundant in most vegetable oils and fish.
- *Monounsaturated* fats are concentrated in olive oil and peanut oil.
- *Saturated* fats are found in animal products and in two vegetable oils, coconut oil and palm oil.

The IDEAL Eating Plan will help you to reduce your total fat intake and to emphasize the unsaturated selections. Recent studies have demonstrated that monounsaturated fats may be the best fat choice, possibly helping to prevent heart disease and other chronic ills. Special fatty acids found mainly in fish ("omega-3" fatty acids) might also help to prevent heart disease, stroke, and certain cancers. Thus, the IDEAL Eating Plan includes the healthiest food sources of fat (e.g., olive oil, natural peanut butter, fish and shellfish) in moderate amounts.

The high-fat foods lists that follow can be turned into a handy poster: Make a photocopy to post on your refrigerator door or on one of your kitchen cabinets for planning a meal or easy scrutiny when you are reaching for a snack.

FOODS HIGH IN SATURATED FAT

Butter

Chips—corn, potato

Cheese—whole milk

Chocolate, cocoa butter

Coconut

Crackers—butter or cheese

Cream—light, heavy, half and
half

Creamer, nondairy

Cream cheese

Fatty meats—bacon, burgers,
choice grades, cold cuts, hot
dogs, marbled meats, prime
cuts, sausages, scrapple,
spareribs

French fries

Fried foods—chicken, fish,
meats, potatoes, vegetables

Granola, commercial

Ice cream

Lard

Margarine, stick

Meat drippings and gravies

Milk—whole

Oils—coconut, palm,
hydrogenated vegetable

Pastries and baked goods—
croissants, Danish, doughnuts,
quick breads, cakes, cookies,
pies

Salt pork

Shortening

Sour cream

FOODS HIGH IN POLY- OR MONOUNSATURATED FATS

Avocado

Fish and shellfish

Margarine—soft

Mayonnaise

Nuts

Oils—corn, cottonseed, safflower, sesame, soybean, sunflower,
rapeseed (canola), olive, peanut

Olives

Peanut butter—natural

Salad dressings made with oils listed above

Sesame and sunflower seeds

Sesame butter, tahini

THE CHOLESTEROL CURE

Concern about cholesterol is certainly in vogue right now, the target of medical and media attention. Cholesterol is actually a fatlike substance found in all body tissues. Although your liver manufactures most of the cholesterol found in your body, the process is partly regulated by your diet. Fat, notably *saturated* fat, plays the most influential role. Since an elevated level of blood cholesterol puts you at an increased risk for a heart attack or stroke, keeping your blood cholesterol down by keeping your fat intake low is a wise idea. Three other lifestyle factors which can influence blood cholesterol levels are being overweight, consuming foods high in cholesterol, and not exercising. The IDEAL Weight-Loss Program tackles all of these risk factors by providing:

- A low-fat eating plan that is low in saturated fat and cholesterol
- An exercise plan that most anyone can follow
- An effective way to lose excess weight—and keep it off

The first list that follows indicates common foods high in fat *and* cholesterol. The second list indicates (better) food choices that are low in fat yet still rich in cholesterol. Your IDEAL Eating Plan will help you to moderate your intakes from both lists.

HIGH-FAT, CHOLESTEROL-RICH FOODS

Animal fats	Cream cheese
Fatty meats—bacon, burgers, choice grades, cold cuts, hot dogs, marbled meats, prime cuts, sausages, scrapple, spareribs	Eggs
	Eggnog
	Ice cream
	Lard
	Liver
Butter	Milk—whole
Caviar	Organ meats—brains, gizzards, heart, kidney, sweetbreads
Cheese—whole milk	
Cream—light, heavy, half and half	Salt pork
	Sour cream

LOW-FAT, CHOLESTEROL-RICH FOODS
(Limit intakes in accordance with your eating plan)

Crab	Lean meats	Shrimp

THE BULK OF YOUR DIET

The Dietary Guidelines recommend that you emphasize foods high in starch and fiber. By choosing foods that are good sources of complex carbohydrates—whole-grain breads and cereals, pasta, potatoes, beans, and peas—you will obtain plenty of starch and dietary fiber. The starch serves as a nutritious low-fat source of energy, and the fiber provides you with bulk. Most Americans consume diets that are very low in bulk, which contributes to common digestive complaints, including constipation and hemorrhoids.

There are several different kinds of fiber, each with different physical properties and health effects. Foods high in the "soluble" forms of fiber—oat bran, fruits and vegetables, peas and beans—slow down the rate of absorption and help to reduce blood cholesterol. Foods rich in "insoluble" fibers—wheat bran and whole grains—speed up digestion, so play a preventive role in digestive diseases and (possibly) certain cancers. By including a variety of high-fiber foods in your diet, you can enjoy all of these health benefits. And by emphasizing the *low-fat* fibrous foods, you can fill up without filling out.

The lists that follow illustrate the best food sources of fiber and identity the low-fat choices. These foods form the bulk of the IDEAL Eating Plan.

HIGH-FIBER, LOW-FAT FOODS

Bran	Fig cookies
Bran cereals	Oat bran
Whole-grain breads	Popcorn—plain, no oil
Whole-grain cereals	Brown rice
Whole-grain crackers	Wild rice

Fruits—especially apples, berries, grapes, peaches, pears, plums, and dried fruits

Vegetables—especially broccoli, brussels sprouts, cabbage, carrots, cauliflower, corn, dried peas and beans, greens, and potatoes (with the skin)

HIGH-FIBER, HIGH-FAT FOODS

Bran muffins*
Granola
Nuts

Peanut butter, natural
Wheat germ

---

*See accompanying box for a high-fiber, *low-fat* bran muffin recipe.

STEVE'S IDEAL OAT BRAN MUFFINS

Here's one of my own favorite recipes for high-fiber, *low-fat* oat bran muffins, a healthful and tasty alternative to the commercial versions that are loaded with hidden fats.

1 cup hot oat bran cereal, uncooked
1 cup whole-wheat flour
¼ cup firmly packed brown sugar
1 Tbsp. baking powder

8 oz. plain nonfat yogurt
¼ cup skim milk
1 egg, beaten slightly
¼ cup honey
1 Tbsp. vegetable oil
½ cup raisins or chopped dates

1. Heat oven to 425° F.
2. In a mixing bowl, stir together cereal, flour, sugar, and baking powder.
3. In a separate bowl, mix yogurt with milk. Add egg, honey, and oil; blend batter well.
4. Stir dry ingredients into batter, mixing until just moistened. Do not overbeat.
5. Stir in dried fruit.
6. Fill paper-lined muffin tins three-quarters full. Bake 15 to

20 minutes, or until golden brown and toothpick inserted in centers comes clean.

Yields 12 muffins with ½ teaspoon fat per muffin

SWEET AND SALTY

The typical American diet includes over one hundred and twenty-five pounds of sugar a year! For some of us, this is equivalent to consuming our own weight in sugar! Since the simple carbohydrates found in fruits, vegetables, and milk can provide us with plenty of natural sugar, the rest is "extra." Your body has no need for this extra sugar. Sweet foods tend to be too high in fat, too low in nutritional value, and far too easy to overconsume.

We are born with an innate taste for sweets. The key to healthy eating is not to try to eliminate all sugar, but to learn to select *nutritious low-fat sweets* instead of the heavyweights. The IDEAL Eating Plan does not exclude your favorite sweets, but following the program can help you to reduce your intake to moderate amounts (as I have done).

Another dietary culprit on your dinner table, sitting there right next to the sugar bowl, is the salt shaker. Although sugar is not usually a *direct* cause of ill health, salt *can* be a factor in heart disease. For the one out of every three Americans who suffers from hypertension (high blood pressure), about one-third are "salt sensitive," making an immoderate salt intake dangerous. And some people respond to excessive salt intake with uncomfortable fluid retention and bloating. Most foods are natural sources of sodium (salt is sodium chloride), so we can obtain adequate amounts of this essential mineral without lifting the salt shaker. Processed foods and convenience and fast foods tend to be too high in sodium to be healthful (and are often high in fat as well).

On the IDEAL Eating Plan, you can gradually reduce your taste for salty foods, resulting in a more healthful sodium intake. It's amazingly easy.

The first two lists that follow indicate common sugar-rich and sodium-rich foods that are also high in fat. Note how *long* these two lists are, and notice how few of the selections are *not* processed foods. The final two lists show you some low-fat alternatives for sweets and salty foods.

HIGH-FAT, SUGAR-RICH FOODS

CAKES:
Cake mixes
Cheesecakes
Chocolate and devil's food cake
Commercial cakes
Cupcakes
Fruitcakes
Snack cakes

CANDY:
Candy with fillings, nuts, nougat, caramel
Caramel popcorn
Chocolates and chocolate bars

COOKIES:
Bakery cookies
Commercial cookies
Frozen cookies (heat 'n serve)

CEREALS:
Granola

DRINKS:
Eggnogs
Milkshakes

FROZEN DESSERTS:
Frozen tofu
Ice cream
Ice milk

PASTRIES:

Danish
Doughnuts
Pies
Poptarts

YOGURT:

Flavored or fruited whole-milk
   yogurt
Frozen whole-milk yogurt

HIGH-FAT, SODIUM-RICH FOODS

MEATS:

Bacon
Canned meats, chipped beef,
   corned beef, stews
Cold cuts, hot dogs, sausage,
   scrapple
Dried meats, smoked meats, ham,
   pastrami

FISH:

Canned fish in oil (unless low-
   sodium)
Caviar
Herring, sardines, smoked fish
Lox

VEGETABLES:

Olives
Seasoned vegetables frozen in
   sauces

BREADS:

Biscuits
Commercial baked goods
Crackers (unless unsalted)

SNACK FOODS:

Chips (unless unsalted)
Commercial peanut butter
Commercial popcorn
Dips
Nuts (unless unsalted)
Seeds (unless unsalted)

MISCELLANEOUS:

Canned and dehydrated soups
Canned dinners and packaged
  meals
Fast foods
Frozen dinners
Packaged mixes
Tartar sauce

LOW-FAT, SWEETS

CAKES:

Angel food cake
Sponge cake

CANDY:

Chewing gum
Cough drops, breath mints
Marshmallows

COOKIES:

Fig bars
Gingersnaps
Graham crackers

CEREALS:

Instant hot cereals, flavored
Presweetened breakfast cereals*

DRINKS:

Fruit drinks
Soft drinks
Tonic water

FROZEN DESSERTS:

Frozen fruit bars
Frozen low-fat yogurt
Popsicles
Sherbet
Sorbet

YOGURT:

Flavored or fruited low-fat yogurt
Low-fat yogurt drinks (kefir)

MISCELLANEOUS:

Canned fruit in syrup
Gelatin, flavored
Jams, jellies, preserves

---

*Breakfast cereals containing less than 10 percent sugar include Puffed Rice, Puffed Wheat, Shredded Wheat, Cheerios, Corn Chex, Wheat Chex, Cornflakes, Nutri-Grain, Grape Nuts, Grape Nut Flakes, Total, Wheaties.

**Sugars—brown, confectioners',
    granulated, raw
Sweeteners—corn syrup, corn
    sweeteners, honey, maple
    syrup, mollasses, sorghum

**Hidden sugars can be detected by scanning labels for corn sweeteners, corn syrup, dextrose, fructose, galactose, glucose, invert sugar, maltose, sucrose, "natural sweeteners".

LOW-FAT, SALTY FOODS

FISH:

Canned fish, in water (unless low-
    sodium)
Canned tuna, in water (unless low-
    sodium)
Ocean fish
Shellfish

VEGETABLES:

Canned vegetables (unless low-so-
    dium)
Pickled vegetables
Pickles
Sauerkraut
Tomato juice
Vegetable cocktail

BREADS:

Breadsticks (unless low-sodium)
Low-fat crackers (unless unsalted)
Pretzels (unless low-sodium)

CONDIMENTS:

Catsup
Cooking wine
Horseradish, prepared
Meat extracts, marinades, tenderizers
Prepared mustard
Relishes
Sauces—barbecue, chili, steak, soy, Worcestershire
*Salts—celery, garlic, kosher, onion, sea, seasoned, table

MISCELLANEOUS:

Bouillon (unless low-sodium)
Canned broths
Vegetable extract

*Scan labels for hidden salt in the form of baking soda/sodium bicarbonate, baking powder, brine, monosodium glutamate (MSG), soda, sodium, sodium chloride; smaller amounts also found in disodium phosphate and sodium-saccharin, sodium alginate, sodium sulfite, sodium benzoate, sodium propionate, sodium hydroxide.

DRINK DEFENSIVELY

Since alcohol is so much a part of our social customs, we tend to overlook the nutritional consequences of "having a few drinks." Sometimes we actually "forget" that several pints of ale, a bottle of fine wine, or those cocktail hour martinis contribute a significant amount of calories to our daily intake. Alcohol is *not* a good source of nutrients, plus it acts as a diuretic in the body, depleting you of essential fluids and minerals.

So what can we party animals—or wine connoisseurs or typical social drinkers—do? Be moderate. The IDEAL Eating Plan does not prohibit alcoholic beverages for those who drink, but it encourages you to limit your intake to a healthful amount. This may also help you to eliminate "happy hour" overeating, which is caused by the relaxation of inhibitions that can accompany alcohol intake.

For some, curbing alcohol consumption alone will lead to loss of excess weight. And there are plenty of new reduced-alcohol and alcohol-free beverages to choose from when you follow the program.

By following this eating plan, you will be adhering to the U.S. government's "Dietary Guidelines for Americans." You will also be consuming a diet that meets the current recommendations of the U.S. Surgeon General, the American Heart Association, the American Cancer Society, the American Diabetes Association, the American Dietetic Association, and most health professionals. Plus you will be eating in a way that satisfies your own *personal* tastes and needs. In combination with a program of regular exercise, you can't lose healthwise!

NOT DIETING IS THE IDEAL DIET

When I first began to investigate the field of nutrition a dozen years ago, there was much I needed to learn. And now, with the ever increasing findings of nutrition research and almost daily dietary discoveries, there is an overwhelming amount of information flooding in. Now you can take advantage of the latest scientific findings—and my years of self-experimentation—in order to lose weight *and* eat well. In the next two chapters, I will provide you with practical advice on the equipment and techniques you will need in order to select and prepare low-fat foods. Once you know how easy it can be to eat the IDEAL way, you can stop dieting and lose weight in the same healthful manner that I did.

CHAPTER

9

IDEAL Food Selection: Fat Slashing

*W*hen I first began to change my diet to achieve a better balance, I was worried that I would have to give up all of my beloved dining-out spots. Not true. Gradually, with careful experimentation, I learned how to make healthy food choices in all of my favorite eating establishments. Now I'll show you how you can do the same.

To my surprise, I also began to enjoy preparing my own low-fat meals at home. I know the kinds of foods I should buy, and I understand how to decipher package labels when required. Now I'll share these insights with you.

Everything you need to know in order to select and prepare low-fat foods and thereby follow the IDEAL Eating Plan permanently and palatably has been included in this chapter and the one that follows. What this book does *not* include are detailed calorie counts for foods, day-by-day menu plans with the usual low-calorie recipes, and the typical restricted diet for you to go on—and off. If you have Diet-Induced Overweight, you already know (all too well) how to go on—and off—a diet. You can automatically reel off the caloric contents for most foods without even consulting a reference book. You've tried all of those diets, and ultimately they've failed you. This time you are learning to *take control.*

DETECTING HIDDEN FATS

Did you know that the calories in fat, those approximate 9 calories per gram of fat, are not the same as the calories in protein and carbohydrate? Not only are there more than twice as many calories *by weight* in fat as in protein and carbohydrate (which have only about 4 calories per gram each), but fat calories are handled differently by the body. Recent research has demonstrated that excess food fat calories are more efficiently stored as body fat. This means that whenever you eat foods high in fat, the calories (which are ample, since fat is naturally high in calories) are easily converted by the body into the storage form of energy— that is, overweight, excess body fat. And, since the adult nutritional requirement for fat is minimal, we can reduce the amount of fat in our diets to a *moderate intake* without jeopardizing our health.

In order to be able to reduce the fat content of your diet to a healthy and weight-loss promoting level, you will need to become skilled at recognizing food fat sources. Sometimes this is obvious—a pool of butter on top of your pile of mashed potatoes, a wedge of white fat on the end of your pork chop. Other times, it requires the ability to detect hidden fat, as in those tempting sweet baked goods, which are also surprisingly high in fat calories.

To make your task easier, I will equip you with a handy Fat Counter providing the total fat in grams and in teaspoons in everyday foods. When you adopt the particular phase of the IDEAL Eating Plan that is appropriate for you, the Fat Counter can help you to make the best food selections every day, until doing so eventually becomes second nature for you.

When I first began to reduce the fat in my diet, I often needed to be able to evaluate the fat content in food choices I was trying to make. It was downright bothersome to continuously consult bulky nutrient-value books and charts that list the total grams of fat in common foods. Moreover, *grams* of fat seemed too impractical for me to visualize. And then I stumbled across a wonderful little cookbook published by the Oregon Division of the American Cancer Society: *Simply Nutritious* (see Appendix B for ordering information). It provided the solution to my fat tallying woes in the form of a Fat Counter, with the total fat content for everyday foods given in grams *and in teaspoons*. With the generous permission of the American Cancer Society, I have included in this chapter my own revised and expanded version of their handy chart.

In my Fat Counter, everyday foods are divided into the appropriate basic food groups, with fats listed last. Additional "extra" foods—those items that tend to provide more calories than nutrients—are provided in three separate Fat Counter charts: "A Fat Look at Snack Foods," "A Fat Look at Fast Foods," and "A Fat Look at Convenience Foods." Alcohol does not contain fat, so has not been included in the Fat Counter.

Note that the foods in each section have been listed in descending order of fat content. This makes it easier to compare foods within each food group to find the choices lowest in fat—in grams or, for more practical visualization, in teaspoons. For foods with less than ¼ teaspoon of fat, the amount can be considered to be negligible ("—"). The teaspoon equivalents have been rounded off to aid in easy visualization.

You might want to photocopy the Fat Counter charts to post in your kitchen or insert in your IDEAL Log. Until you become really familiar with the fat contents of everyday foods, it is helpful to have the specifics where you can grasp them at a glance.

FAT COUNTER

Food and Amount	Total Fat in Grams	Total Fat in Teaspoons*
FRUITS:		
Coconut—½ cup grated	8.6	1½
All others	0	0

*Values have been rounded off; "—" means less than ¼ teaspoon.

Food and Amount	Total Fat in Grams	Total Fat in Teaspoons*
VEGETABLES:		
Avocado—½ medium	16	3¼
Olives—5 small	4	1
All others	0	0
GRAIN PRODUCTS:		
Granola—½ cup	8	1½
Chow mein noodles—½ cup	6	1¼
Popover—1 average	4–5	1
Pancakes—2 average	4	1
Waffle—1 average	3–4	1
Cornbread—average piece	3.8	¾
Hamburger roll—1	2.2	½
Brown rice—1 cup cooked	0.9	—
Bread, white—1 slice	0.7	—
Bread, whole-wheat—1 slice	0.7	—
Bread, French or Italian—1 slice	0.6	—
Pasta—1 cup cooked	0.5	—
Popcorn, hot-air popped—1½ cups	0.4	—
White rice, cooked—1 cup	0.2	—
Bagel—1	<1	—
Melba toast, matzoh—1	<1	—
MILK:		
Milk, whole—1 cup	9	1¾
Milk, low-fat, 2%—1 cup	5	1
Milk, low-fat, 1%—1 cup	2.6	½
Milk, skim—1 cup	0.4	—
Buttermilk, skim—1 cup	0.4	—
MILK PRODUCTS:		
Whipping cream—½ cup	24	5
Sour cream—½ cup	16	3¼
Half and half—½ cup	16	3¼
Ice cream—½ cup	8–15	1½–3
Yogurt, whole milk—1 cup	8	1½

Food and Amount	Total Fat in Grams	Total Fat in Teaspoons*
Yogurt, low-fat—1 cup	4	1
Kefir—1 cup	3	½
Ice milk—½ cup	2.8	½
Sherbet—½ cup	1.9	¼
Frozen yogurt, low-fat—½ cup	1.5	¼

CHEESE:

Brie, camembert—1 oz.	13–15	2¾–3
Cream cheese—1 oz.	10	2
Hard cheese (cheddar, jack, gruyère, Swiss, etc.)—1 oz.	9–10	2
Neufchâtel—1 oz.	7	1½
Feta—1 oz.	6	1¼
Mozzarella, whole milk—1 oz.	6	1¼
Parmesan, grated—¼ cup	6	1¼
Cream cheese, "light"—1 oz.	5	1
Mozzarella, part-skim—1 oz.	4.5	1
Cottage cheese, creamed, 4.2% fat—½ cup	4.2	1
Ricotta, whole milk—1 oz.	4	1
Lite-Line brand—1 oz.	3	½
Cottage cheese, low-fat, 2%—½ cup	2.2	½
Weight Watchers low-fat brand—1 oz.	2	½
Ricotta, part-skim—1 oz.	2	½

MEAT AND POULTRY:

Ground beef, 25% fat—3 oz.	21.5	4¼
Hot dog—1 average	13	2½
Chicken frankfurter—1 average	12.5	2½
Pork—3 oz.	12	2½
Lamb—3 oz.	12	2½
Salami—1 oz.	10	2
Spareribs—3 small	10	2
Ground beef, 10% fat—3 oz.	8.5	1¾
Beef, sirloin—3 oz.	8.5	1¾
Chicken or turkey, dark meat—3 oz.	8.4	1¾
Bologna, beef—1 oz.	8	1½
Bacon, 2 strips	7.5	1½

Food and Amount	Total Fat in Grams	Total Fat in Teaspoons*
Veal—3 oz.	5	1
Chicken or turkey, light meat—3 oz.	4	1
Turkey cold cuts—1 oz.	1.5	1/4

FISH:

Salmon, chinook—3 oz.	13.3	2⅔
Tuna, in oil—3 oz.	8	1½
Salmon, pink—3 oz.	3.2	¾
Tuna, in water—3 oz.	1	1/4
Shellfish (clams, crab, lobster, oysters, scallops, shrimp, etc.)—3 oz.	0–1	—
White fish (cod, halibut, perch, sole, trout, etc.)—3 oz.	0–1	—

MEAT ALTERNATIVES:

Peanut butter—1 Tbsp.	8	1½
Egg, whole—1	6	1¼
Tofu—3.5 oz.	4.2	1
Egg white—1	0.5	—
Legumes—1 cup	<1	—

NUTS AND SEEDS

Macadamia nuts—1 oz.	23.5	4¾
Pecans—1 oz.	22	4½
Filberts—1 oz.	19.1	4
Peanuts, dry roasted— ¼ cup	17.6	3½
Sunflower seeds—¼ cup	16.8	3¼
Almonds—1 oz.	16.2	3¼
Pistachios—1 oz.	16.1	3¼
Walnuts—1 oz.	15.1	3
Peanuts, in shells—1 oz.	14	3
Cashews—1 oz.	13.1	2¾
Tahini—1 Tbsp.	10	2
Sesame seeds—1 Tbsp.	4.5	1

Food and Amount	Total Fat in Grams	Total Fat in Teaspoons*
FATS:		
Butter—1 Tbsp.	14	3
Oils, all—1 Tbsp.	14	3
Margarine—1 Tbsp.	12	2½
Mayonnaise—1 Tbsp.	11	2¼
Italian dressing, commercial—1 Tbsp.	8.4	1¾
Soft margarine—1 Tbsp.	8	1½
Roquefort dressing, commercial— 1 Tbsp.	7.6	1½
Thousand Island dressing, commercial— 1 Tbsp.	7.6	1½
Sour cream—2 Tbsp.	6	1¼
Heavy cream—1 Tbsp.	5.6	1
French dressing—1 Tbsp.	5.4	1
Cream cheese—1 Tbsp.	5.3	1
Imitation/diet mayonnaise—1 Tbsp.	5	1
Diet margarine—1 Tbsp.	5	1
Nondairy creamer—2 Tbsp.	3	½
Half and half—1 Tbsp.	1.8	¼
Low-calorie dressing, commercial— 1 Tbsp.	1	¼

Adapted and reprinted with permission from the American Cancer Society/Oregon Division, Inc.

A FAT LOOK AT SNACK FOODS

Food and Amount	Total Fat in Grams	Total Fat in Teaspoons*
CHIPS AND POPCORN:		
Potato chips—1 oz.	10–13	2–2¾
Corn chips—1 oz.	10	2
Cheese puffs—1 oz.	10	2
Tortilla chips—1 oz.	7	1¼

*Values have been rounded off; "—" means less than ¼ teaspoon.

Food and Amount	Total Fat in Grams	Total Fat in Teaspoons*
Microwave popcorn— 4 cups, popped	7	1¼
Commercial popcorn— 3–4 cups, popped	6–7	1¼
Pretzels—5 medium or 2 large	1	¼
CRACKERS:		
Goldfish—1 oz.	10	2
Cheese sandwich-type—4	6–7	1¼
Ritz—4	4	1
Triscuits—4	3.5	¾
Stoned wheat—4	2	½
Saltines—4	1–2	½
Wheat thins—4	1.5	¼
Zwieback—1	.4	—
Crispbread or rye crisp—4	.4	—
Matzoh—1	.3	—
Melba toast—2–3	.1	—
Rice cakes—2	.1	—
SWEETS:		
Pecan pie—average slice	20–23	4–4¾
Apple pie, homemade—average slice	13	2½
Pumpkin pie—average slice	11–13	2½
Cake (chocolate, cheese, carrot, etc.)	10–11+	2+
Chocolate bar with nuts—1 average	10–11	2
Chocolate bar—1 average	10	2
Twinkies—2	10	2
Snack cake—1 average	8–10	1¾–2
Pound cake—average slice	7–10	1½–2
Brownie—average	7–10	1½–2
Doughnut, raised	7–10	1½–2

Food and Amount	Total Fat in Grams	Total Fat in Teaspoons*
Doughnut, cakelike	8	1¾
Custard—½ cup	7–8	1½
Reese's peanut butter cups—1	7	1½
Oreos—2	7	1¼
Ice cream sandwich—1	6	1¼
Chocolate chip cookies—2	5–6	1
Poptart—1	5	1
Fudge—2" square	5	1
Granola bar	4–5	1
Flavored puddings—½ cup	3–5	½–1
Gingersnaps—2	3	½
Sponge cake—small serving	2.5–3	½
Fig bars—2	2–2.5	½
Oatmeal raisin cookies—2	1–2	¼
Animal crackers—4	1–2	¼
Graham crackers—2	1–2	¼
Angel food cake	.1	—
Frozen fruit bars	0	0

A FAT LOOK AT FAST FOODS

Food—Average Serving Size	Total Fat in Grams	Total Fat in Teaspoons*
Croissant with ham	42	8¼
Nachos supreme	40	8
Sausage and egg biscuit	35–40	7–8
Whopper	38	7½
Big Mac	35	7
Cheese nachos	35	7
Baked potato, cheese stuffed	34	7

*Values have been rounded off.

Food and Amount	Total Fat in Grams	Total Fat in Teaspoons*
Biscuit with sausage	28–31	5½–6¼
Ham and egg biscuit	26	5¼
Fish sandwich	25–26	5
Chicken breast, fried	24	5
Biscuit with egg	22	4¼
Baked potato, stuffed with broccoli and cheese	22	4¼
Chicken nuggets—6	20	4
Biscuit with ham	18	3½
Hash browns	9–19	2–4
Sausage patty	9–18	2–3½
Onion rings	16–17	3¼
Burrito, beef	16	3¼
Chicken wing, fried	16	3¼
French fries	12–15	2½–3
Danish	12–14	2½–3
Roast beef sandwich	10–15	2–3
Cheeseburger	14	3
Apple pie	12	2½
Taco	11	2
Chocolate shake	10–11	2
Hamburger	10	2
Croissant, plain	10	2
Burrito, bean—large	9	1¾
Bran muffin	6–11 +	1¼–2 +
Corn or fruit muffin	6–9	1¼–1¾
Pepperoni pizza—1 slice	6–7	1¼
Cheese pizza—1 slice	3–4	¾

Note: "Extra crispy" meals are higher in fat; ditto for "supreme"; "special" sauces can add more than 2 teaspoons fat.

A FAT LOOK AT CONVENIENCE FOODS

Food and Amount	Total Fat in Grams	Total Fat in Teaspoons*
VEGETABLES:		
Potato salad, commercial—⅔ cup	15.5	3
Creamed vegetable soups, canned— 1 cup	4–15	1–3
Mashed potato, instant—½ cup	7	1½
Coleslaw, commercial—½ cup	4.4	1
Vegetable soup, canned—1 cup	2–4	½–1
Vegetables in sauces, frozen—½ cup	1–5	¼–1
PASTAS AND BEAN DISHES:		
Macaroni and cheese, box mix— ¾ cup serving	14–17	3–3½
Chili with beans, canned—1 cup	15.5	3
Lasagna, canned—½ 15-oz. can	9	2
Spaghetti, canned—½ 15-oz. can	8	1¾
Ravioli, canned—½ 15-oz. can	5	1
Pork and beans, canned—1 cup	2–8	½–1½
MEAT DISHES:		
TV dinner—average frozen meal	8–35	1½–7
Corned beef hash, canned—½ 15-oz. can	24	5
TV dinner—"light" meal	5–20	1–4
Deviled ham, canned—2 oz.	18	3½
Spam, canned—2 oz.	15	3
Chicken pot pie, frozen—4 oz. serving	12–15	2½–3
Beef stew, canned—½ 15-oz. can	9	2
Turkey pot pie, frozen—4 oz.	8.5	1¾
Beef pot pie, frozen—4 oz.	8	1¾
Meat loaf, frozen—4 oz.	7	1½
Chicken chop suey, canned—7 oz.	4.4	1
Chicken chow mein, canned—6 oz.	2	½

*Values have been rounded off.

Food and Amount	Total Fat in Grams	Total Fat in Teaspoons*
FISH DISHES:		
Tuna salad, commercial—½ cup	10	2
Clam chowder, canned—1 cup	7–8	1½
Fish sticks, frozen—2	5	1
PIZZA:		
Pizza, Weight Watchers frozen— 1 pkg.	14	2¾
Pizza, French bread, frozen—1 serving	13	2½
Pizza, cheese, frozen—2 slices	10–12	2–2½
MISCELLANEOUS:		
Stuffing, box mix—½ cup serving	9	2
Gravy, canned—½ cup	1–4	¼–1

TALLY UP YOUR FAT INTAKE

Let's do a fat tally right now to see how much fat (in teaspoons) you're eating. Be ready to discover a total fat intake that is closer to the average American male or female than to the ideal (see the charts in chapter 7). That's okay, that's why you need to be on the IDEAL Eating Plan! Keep in mind that this will be a *rough estimate* of your fat intake, which varies from day to day and may actually be lower (or higher) than the tally obtained by using the Fat Counter figures.

If you already began keeping track of your daily food intake in your IDEAL Log, select a sample day to tally your fat intake. If you *haven't* been recording your food intake, record in your log everything you can remember eating over the past twenty-four hours. Don't try to make your score look good. The point is to learn what dietary habits need to be changed, so that you can then alter any high-fat eating practices *permanently*.

Use the Fat Counter to total your day's fat intake in teaspoons. If there are foods included in your log that are not given in the Fat Counter, estimate fat content as best you can by comparing with similar foods listed in the charts. Be sure that fat totals represent the actual serving sizes eaten (for example, 2 to 3 teaspoons for an extra large bran muffin, versus the 1¼ to 2 teaspoons for the "average" restaurant size).

So, how did you do? If your fat intake appears high, like the average American fat intake, don't worry. The IDEAL Eating Plan will help you to get a rein on your fat intake—gradually, painlessly, permanently.

You might want to continue to record the food you eat, the fat in teaspoons for each food, and the daily total fat in teaspoons for the first month or so you are on the program. After that, you can spot-check your diet every now and then to detect hidden fats as you continue to eat this way—permanently.

MENU SCANNING

A few years ago, when I entered my first Ironman triathlon, I was about one-third of the way through the bicycle leg of the endurance event when I started to feel hungry. Since my only goal was to *finish* the race, not to win or even score a competitive time, I decided to stop off for lunch when I spied a fast food eatery up the road ahead of me. I quickly ordered a plain burger and a soft drink, which I devoured enthusiastically before continuing on my way.

I achieved my goal and completed the course. Stopping for a hamburger didn't help my finishing time (although I made my objective of finishing under the seventeen-hour deadline), but it illustrates the functional role of fast food restaurants in our society.

On the IDEAL Eating Plan, you *don't* have to forego fast foods. You just need to learn how to scan a menu. For breakfast on the go, instead of automatically ordering high-fat bacon and eggs, Danish pastries, or sausage biscuits, make careful, healthful, low-fat choices from breakfast menus.

IDEAL BREAKFAST CHOICES

Studies indicate that when we are trying to lose weight, the *timing* of meals can be as important as the content. People who skip breakfast tend to weigh more than people who start off the day with a well-balanced meal! And studies indicate that eating a good breakfast can help you to function better during the hours that follow. Night eaters tend to weigh more than people who spread their food intakes more evenly throughout the day.

Obviously, eating breakfast every morning is a good habit to develop. About one-quarter of the population usually skips this meal. Others make it a high-fat habit. It is essential that the foods you choose for your morning menu are low in fat. The Breakfast Items section in the chart below illustrates some ideal home-cooked or fast food breakfast choices.

One of my own favorite breakfasts is hot oatmeal or oat bran cereal topped with fresh fruit—sliced bananas, strawberries, blue-berries, etc. I can make this for myself at home, and most restaurants have some variation available. At some fast food places, fruit juice and an English muffin (unbuttered) may have to suffice. Most eateries serve bran, corn, or fruit muffins these days, but be aware that some of these baked goods are made with more fat than others. Rub your muffin with a paper napkin and observe the grease spot—no need to add more butter to it! And if the muffin you purchase is as big as a grapefruit and as heavy as a baseball, you can bet that it contains more fat than the 2 teaspoons per *average* serving indicated in the Fat Counter! Don't kid yourself, because your body—and your waistline—won't be fooled.

BELLY UP TO THE SALAD BAR

I like to create my own salads, at home as well as at the ubiq-uitous salad bar, now located everywhere from supermarkets to fast food outlets. But these days I scan all potential salad ingredients for fat, selecting only the low-fat options and topping my truly light creations with a low-fat dressing. If a reduced- or low-calorie dressing is unavailable, use vinegar, lemon juice, black pepper, and a tablespoon of cottage cheese to dress your salad. The Salads and Miscellaneous sections of the IDEAL Menu Selections chart illustrate the best low-fat salad choices.

ORDER CREATIVELY

At least at the salad bar, you know that you have *total control* over the vegetable concoction you are about to create and consume. But when you are faced with a limited restaurant menu, does this mean you have no control over your upcoming meal? Fortunately, an old saying can ring true for you in the restaurant setting: "The customer is always right." Learn to be assertive (but nice, not aggressive) when dining out. Tell the waiter or waitress what you want: "Please serve the salad dressing separately, on the side." Ask questions: "Is the fish broiled in butter?" Remember, *they* are there to serve you. And *you* are there to enjoy your meal, which now entails knowing how much fat is in the food you choose to eat—or not eat.

Select restaurants where you feel most in control of your menu choices. Since Americans have become increasingly health and diet conscious, more and more restaurants are catering to their nutritionally concerned customers. A recent Gallup survey found that three out of every four restaurants are willing to meet the health-related requests of their patrons: The chefs will eliminate salt in cooking, serve sauces and salad dressings on the side, use margarine or vegetable oil instead of butter on vegetables and in broiling meats or fish, remove the skin from poultry prior to baking, provide whole-grain breads, and offer plain fresh fruit for dessert. (For a guide to restaurants offering low-fat menu selections in your area, contact the nearest affiliate of the American Heart Association and request the regional issue of their brochure "Dining Out: A Guide to Restaurant Dining.") Even the airlines now offer low-fat meals, available to travelers who request a special menu twenty-four hours in advance. Try a fruit plate for lunch or a broiled seafood platter on an evening flight. Be sure to call in your order the day before your trip.

It used to be next to impossible to eat well while on the road. No more. Healthy foods are big business now, so hotels, restaurants, and airlines are meeting consumer demands. But it is still up to you to make the best food choices possible, selecting the most nutritious low-fat menu items available. Use the IDEAL Menu Selections chart below and your Fat Counter to assist you in dining out healthfully. Whether you are thousands of miles away from home in a gourmet restaurant or around the corner at your local burger joint, this way you *can* eat well.

IDEAL MENU SELECTIONS

IDEAL Choices	Eat in Moderation Only	Beware—High in Fat
BREAKFAST ITEMS:		
Fresh fruit	Fruit in syrup	Biscuits
Fruit juices	English muffins	Cinnamon buns
Bran cereal	Bran, corn, or fruit	Sticky buns
Whole-grain ready-to-	muffins	Croissants
eat cereals	Quick breads (e.g.,	Danish
Oatmeal	banana)	Doughnuts
Other whole-grain	Scones	French toast
cooked cereals	Pancakes with syrup	Granola
Bagels	Waffles with syrup	Hash browns
Whole-wheat English	Low-fat milk	Home fries
muffins	Egg—boiled or poached	Eggs—fried or
Whole-grain toast	Coffee	scrambled
Skim milk	Tea	Omelets
Low-fat yogurt		Bacon and sausage
		Butter or margarine
		Cream or nondairy
		creamers
		Cream cheese
APPETIZERS:		
Fresh fruit	Light fruit soups	Artichokes with drawn
Crudités	Vegetable juices	butter
Gazpacho	Vegetable soups	Seafood with drawn
Escargot	Bean soups	butter
Seafood cocktail	Bouillon or consommé	Chowders
Steamed clams		Creamed soups

IDEAL Choices	Eat in Moderation Only	Beware—High in Fat
Oysters or cherrystone clams		French onion soup
		Soups with cheese or meat
		Pâté

SALADS:

IDEAL Choices	Eat in Moderation Only	Beware—High in Fat
Garden or tossed	Antipasto (lean meats only)	Mayonnaise-based (e.g., egg, chicken, ham or other meats, tunafish, seafood)
Spinach (no bacon)	Caesar's	
Lemon juice	Chef's (lean meats only)	
Vinegar	Low-calorie dressings (on the side)	Coleslaw
	Olive oil (small amounts)	Potato salad
		Commercial dressings
		Croûtons or bacon bits

BREADS AND ROLLS:

IDEAL Choices	Eat in Moderation Only	Beware—High in Fat
French bread	White bread	Garlic bread
Italian bread	Cornbread	Biscuits
Pita bread	Dinner rolls	Buttered rolls
Whole-grain bread	Hard rolls	Croissants
Whole-grain rolls	Submarine rolls	Popovers
Whole-grain crackers	Breadsticks	Sticky buns
Matzoh, melba toast	Crackers	Sweet rolls
Rice cakes	Tortillas, flour (soft)	Butter crackers (e.g., Ritz)
Tortillas, corn		Cheese crackers (e.g., Goldfish)
		Chow mein noodles
		Fried tortillas

VEGETABLES:

IDEAL Choices	Eat in Moderation Only	Beware—High in Fat
All, plain	Seasoned	Avocado
Raw or steamed	Stir-fried	Breaded and fried
		Creamed
		French fried
		Sauced
		Tempura

IDEAL Choices	Eat in Moderation Only	Beware—High in Fat
POTATOES:		
Baked	Candied sweet potatoes	Fried
Boiled		French fries
With low-fat yogurt		Hash browns
		Home fries
		Mashed
		Scalloped
		Stuffed (cheese, etc.)
		Potato salad
		Potato skins
		With butter, gravy, or sour cream
PASTA AND RICE:		
Unadorned whole-grain pastas	White pasta—spaghetti, noodles, etc.—plain or with tomato sauce	Egg noodles
Brown rice		Pasta with cheese, cream, meat sauce
Wild rice	Vegetable pastas	Fried rice
	Saffron or seasoned rice	
	White rice	
	Rice pilaf	
*MEAT, POULTRY, AND FISH:		
Vegetable dishes with lean meats as "condiments"	Lean beef, well trimmed	Ground beef
	Select cuts, "extra lean"	Prime cuts, marbled
	Lean veal	Cuts, cold cuts
Skinless chicken, light meat	Organ meats	Hot dogs
	Wild game	Ham and pork
Skinless turkey, light meat	Anchovies	Lamb
	Sardines	Fried
Clams, mussels, oysters	Marinated fish	Gravies
White fish	Caviar	Hash
	Crab	Parmigiana
	Shrimp	Potpies and stews

*IDEAL choices are baked, boiled, broiled, poached, steamed, stir-fried, or shishkebab.

IDEAL Choices	Eat in Moderation Only	Beware—High in Fat
		Sauces
		Stuffed
		Domestic duck and goose
		Sausages
		Shishkebab

MEAT ALTERNATIVES:

IDEAL Choices	Eat in Moderation Only	Beware—High in Fat
Baked beans, vegetarian	Bean soups	Falafel
Meatless chili	Bean burrito	Nachos
Black beans and rice	Bean tostada	Eggs—fried or scrambled
Red beans and rice	Tofu dishes	Omelets
Hummus	Egg—boiled or poached	Egg sandwiches
Low-fat cottage cheese	Cottage cheese, creamed	Quiches
	Peanuts—dry roasted	Soufflés
	Peanut butter	Nuts

DESSERTS:

IDEAL Choices	Eat in Moderation Only	Beware—High in Fat
Fresh fruit	Lichee nuts	Rich sweets (you know what they are!)
Baked or poached fruit	Fruited or flavored low-fat yogurt	
	Frozen low-fat yogurt	
	Sherbet and sorbet	
	Angel food cake	
	Sponge cake	

BEVERAGES:

IDEAL Choices	Eat in Moderation Only	Beware—High in Fat
Fruit juices	Vegetable juices	Whole milk
Skim milk	Low-fat milk	Chocolate milk
Club soda	Coffee or tea	Milkshakes
Mineral water	Light beer or nonalcoholic beer	Eggnog
	Dry wines	Drinks with whole milk or cream
	Diet soft drinks	

IDEAL Choices	Eat in Moderation Only	Beware—High in Fat

MISCELLANEOUS—ON SALADS OR IN SANDWICHES AND PREPARED DISHES:

IDEAL Choices	Eat in Moderation Only	Beware—High in Fat
Bean sprouts	Barbecue sauce	Avocado
Black pepper	Cocktail sauce	Bacon
Jalapeño pepper	Condiments—sugar,	Bacon bits
Raw vegetables	salt, honey, catsup,	Butter or margarine
Lemon juice	mustard, relish,	Cheeses
Low-fat yogurt	pickles, horseradish	Chips and dips
Vinegar	Hot sauce or salsa	Chocolate
	Tomato sauce	Chocolate chips
	Low-calorie salad	Coconut
	dressings	Cream or nondairy
	Olive oil (*small* amounts)	creamers
		Cream cheese
		Croûtons
		Guacamole
		Mayonnaise
		Olives
		Nuts
		Regular salad dressings
		Sauces—Bearnaise, cheese, cream, Hollandaise, meat, white
		"Special" sauces
		Sour cream
		Sunflower seeds
		Tartar sauce
		Whipped cream

WHEN YOU SHOP, SCAN THE LABEL

Healthy, low-fat eating actually begins in the supermarket. When you examine a food label, there are four main points to consider. I call these your LABEL TARGETS:

1. Fats in the ingredients list—types and position in the list (i.e., relative amount in the food)

2. Fats on the nutrition label (when provided)—grams and whether saturated or unsaturated (when indicated)
3. Other ingredients worth noting (for example, whole grains, sugars, salt/sodium, additives)
4. Additional nutrition information of interest (such as milligrams of cholesterol, grams of sugar versus fiber, milligrams of sodium, calories per serving)

Whenever a diet-related or health claim is made on a food label, the Food and Drug Administration's standard "nutrition information" panel must be provided on the product. This means that if a label says "low in calories" or "no cholesterol," the product must display nutrition information as proof. Be sure to check up on all nutrition claims, however, as they can be highly misleading. For example, a product labeled "no animal fat" can still be high in *vegetable* fat.

Food products with added nutrients (that is, fortified or enriched) also must provide the standard nutrition information. Approximately one-half of the packaged foods available in today's market have a nutrition information panel. This makes it easier (but it's still not all that easy!) to scan for Label Targets 2 and 4.

Most consumers today read food labels. Unfortunately, most of us don't really understand what we're reading. I used to look at the calories per serving, and that was it for the "nutrition" label! Let me show you the easiest method I know for deciphering food labels to your advantage:

1. Scan the ingredients list for fat. Ingredients are listed in order of predominance by *weight*. If fat(s) are first and/or close to the top of the list, you can bet that you've got a high-fat food in hand. Take note of the type of fat. The following terms are used to indicate use of saturated vegetable fats, the least healthful type: *vegetable fat, vegetable shortening, hydrogenated fat, vegetable oil* (unidentified), *hydrogenated vegetable oil, partially hydrogenated vegetable oil, cocoa butter, coconut oil, palm oil, palm kernel oil.*

2. Scan the nutrition information label for fat in grams. Since fat in teaspoons is not provided, you may want to translate the grams into a more practical number, that is, the *number of calories from fat:* number of grams fat × 9 = number of calories from fat.

And if you want to note the *percentage of calories from fat:* number of calories from fat ÷ number of calories per serving × 100 = percent of calories from fat. If you have a head for figures, you'll be able to handle these computations quickly without causing a major traffic jam in the supermarket aisle. If you're not much of a math whiz, refer to your Fat Counter for the approximate fat in teaspoons instead. (And compare to your daily quota: Is the product too high in fat for you to include in your eating plan?) This saves me a lot of supermarket aisle frustration, and helps me to focus on fat instead of calories.

3. *Scan the ingredients list for items high in cholesterol, fiber, sugar, and/or sodium.* By noting where any substances high in these items appear on the ingredients list, you can then determine whether the food is an ideal choice for you. Look for the term *100% whole,* or at least *whole,* when wheat and other grains are listed as major ingredients. And be sure to scan for the alternate terms for sugar and salt (see charts on pages 170 and 171). I usually regard labels touting more than a half dozen ingredients with an extra dose of skepticism, especially when most of the terms are unfamiliar chemical names.

4. *If there are nutrients other than fat of interest to you, scan the nutrition information panel for specifics.* If you must, check for calories per serving. Note that the product "serving size" may not be what *you* would consider a normal portion.

Listed in the box below are some common food labeling terms with their legal definitions. And for those without legal definitions, I've given my own definitions.

DEFINED LABEL TERMS

FOR CALORIES:

- "Light"—has no legal definition (see list of "undefined terms" below)
- "Low-calorie"—has under 40 calories per serving
- "Reduced calorie"—has at least one-third fewer calories than the regular item

FOR CHOLESTEROL:

- "Cholesterol-free"—has less than 2 milligrams per serving
- "Low-cholesterol"—has less than 20 milligrams per serving
- "Reduced cholesterol"—has at least 25 percent less cholesterol than the regular item

FOR FAT IN BEEF:

- "Extra lean"—contains less than 5 percent fat
- "Lean"—contains less than 10 percent fat
- "Light"—contains at least 25 percent less fat than regular beef
- "Lower fat"—contains at least 25 percent less fat than regular beef

FOR FAT IN MILK:

- "Whole"—contains 3.5 percent fat
- "Low-fat (2%)"—contains 2 percent fat
- "Low-fat (1%)"—contains 1 percent fat
- "Nonfat" or "skim"—contains 0.1 percent fat (virtually fat-free)

FOR FAT IN CHEESES (see pages 185–187)

FOR SODIUM:

- "Sodium-free"—contains less than 5 milligrams per serving
- "Very low sodium"—contains less than 35 milligrams per serving
- "Low-sodium"—contains less than 140 milligrams per serving
- "Reduced sodium"—contains at least 75 percent less sodium than the regular item
- "Unsalted"—no salt added (does *not* indicate sodium-free)

FOR GENERAL REFERENCE:

- "U.S. RDA"—a condensed version of the Recommended Dietary Allowances, the estimated amounts of various nutrients needed to maintain good health; the basic *minimum* required for eight essential nutrients out of the forty-plus required daily
- "Enriched"—an indication that some of the nutrients lost in processing have been replaced
- "Fortified"—made with added vitamins and minerals, often not found in the unfortified form
- "Imitation"—a standardized processed food with reduced caloric content and possibly less fat

---

"UNDEFINED" LABEL TERMS

- "Light" or "Lite"—Read the nutrition information label very carefully. Use of this meaningless term is a signal for you to read between the lines to see whether the item is significantly lower in calories, fat, sugar, and/or salt or is simply less dark than comparable products.
- "Sugarless" or "Sugar-free"—No table sugar added. This means that the product *can* contain other forms of sugar such as fructose or dextrose, and that it can still promote tooth decay. Use of either term is definitely no guarantee of a low-fat or low-calorie product.
- "Natural"—Another signal to read between the lines. "Natural" meats and poultry are indeed minimally processed and free of artificial ingredients, but other products are not legally required to meet these same standards. Many "natural" foods are highly processed, made with additives, and notable sources of fat.

> • "Healthy" or "Health Food"—Read, read, read! Lack of legal definition for this term has spawned the misleading labeling of a host of food products high in fat, sugar, salt, and artificial ingredients.

HOW TO READ BETWEEN THE LINES

The food label diagram that follows illustrates how to read a typical food label (in this case, a "health" cereal). Take note of the Label Targets (numbers 1, 2, 3, and 4). And see how you can read between the lines to evaluate a food product *before* you buy it.

	Label Information	Comment
	All-Natural	No legal meaning, so product may contain additives and/or preservatives.
	Health	No legal meaning either, so read between the lines: Read the ingredients list and nutrition information panel.
Cereal		
Label Targets 2 & 4	NUTRITION INFORMATION	
	Serving size 1 oz.	This can be less than ¼ cup if product is dense or heavy.
	Servings per package 10	
	Calories 150	This figure has a 20% leeway, so this product may have from 120 to 180 calories per serving.
	Protein 2 g	
	Carbohydrate** 24 g	Is this complex or simple? See below** to find out.

Label Information		Comment
Fat	5 g	Is this saturated fat? Read INGREDIENTS to find out.
Cholesterol	0 g	No cereal contains cholesterol until milk is added.
Sodium	270 mg.	May not be provided, as listing is optional unless a sodium claim is made.
PERCENTAGE OF US RDA		These 8 nutrients must be listed; others are optional unless a specific claim is made.
Protein	4	
Vitamin A	*	Fortified cereals may
Vitamin C	*	contain 100 % of the US
Thiamin	8	RDA for vitamins and
Riboflavin	2	minerals.
Niacin	2	
Calcium	2	
Iron	2	
*Contains less than 2% of the US RDA for this nutrient.		This is low, but anything less than 10% is actually a meager contribution.
**CARBOHYDRATE INFORMATION		When available, delineates starch versus sugars, plus fiber contents.
Starch & related carbohydrates	10 g	
Sugar	24 g	Best choices contain 2 grams sugar (10% total calories) or less.
Dietary fiber	2 g	High fiber cereals contain 3–4 grams of fiber or more per serving.

Label Targets 1 & 3

INGREDIENTS: Whole wheat, cracked wheat, brown sugar,	Listed in decreasing order of predominance by weight. Check for "whole" grains. Check how close sugars are

Label Information	Comment
corn syrup, salt, vegetable oil (may contain one or more of the following: soybean, hydrogenated palm and/or coconut oil), natural flavors, artificial flavors, yellow no. 5	to the top of the list. Ditto salt/sodium. Since palm and coconut oils are less expensive, these are usually the vegetable oils used in processing; partially hydrogenated oils can be anywhere from 5 to 60% saturated. Specific names for flavorings and spices need not be listed. Except for the indicated dye, specific colors need not be listed.
March 30, 1989	Freshness date.
Ctn. No. X	Recall code.

FOOD ADDITIVES

It is certainly not easy to decipher food labels and evaluate ingredient lists, but an understanding of the most common chemical additives can be of some assistance. The chart that follows describes the major types of additives, their functions, and uses in processed food products.

Type of Additive— Examples	Functions	Common Usage
Nutrients: • Vitamins • Minerals	Replace nutrients lost in processing (enrich) or add nutrients (fortify)	Enriched flour, bread, rice; fortified or enriched cereals; milk, margarine, salt
Preservatives: • Nitrates, nitrites • Sulfites • Benzoic acid • Calcium propionate	Prevent spoilage, extend shelf life, or protect aroma and/or flavor	Many processed foods, including luncheon meats, canned dips, frozen potatoes, bread, and baked goods

Type of Additive— Examples	Functions	Common Usage
Anti-oxidants: • Ascorbic acid • Citric acid • BHA, BHT	Prevent or delay spoilage	Many preserved foods, including ready-to-eat cereals, crackers, canned vegetables, and soft drinks
Leavening agents: • Baking soda • Baking powder	Affect texture and volume	Baked goods
Emulsifiers: • Monoglycerides • Diglycerides • Lecithin • Polysorbate	Improve consistency, stability, texture	Baked goods, frozen desserts, salad dressings, puddings, gelatin
Stabilizers, thickeners, texturizers: • Carrageenan • Gums • Pectin • Cellulose • Gelatin • Food starch	Improve texture and consistency, give body	Baked goods, prepared desserts, soups, other packaged foods
pH-control agents: • Acetic, citric, other acids • Phosphates, other buffers	Control acidity/ alkalinity for texture and taste	Soft drinks, baked goods
Sweeteners: • Natural sugars • Artificial sweeteners	Improve sweetness	Candy, baked goods, soft drinks, fruit drinks, many processed foods
Flavors: • Artificial flavors • Natural Flavors	Improve or restore flavor lost in processing	Baked goods, cereals, packaged foods, many processed foods
Flavor enhancers: • MSG	Modify flavor	Gravies, canned foods, soups

Type of Additive— Examples	Functions	Common Usage
Colors: • Annatto • Carotene • Caramel • Saffron • Synthetic colors	Improve or alter color to increase appeal	Almost all processed foods, from ice cream, butter and margarine, to dark bread, seasoned rice, canned and frozen fruit

Note that the first set of additives improve the quality and add nutrients to foods. The second set of additives maintain food quality but are only used in processed products, not in fresh, natural foods. The third set of chemicals aid in processing and enhance consumer appeal but, again, are only used in processed foodstuffs. Chemical additives from the last grouping are used solely to enhance consumer appeal: We like our butter to look yellow, our strawberry ice cream to taste like sweet strawberries. The bottom three groupings of food additives include chemicals of questionable safety. Usually, the shorter the ingredients list and the more familiar the ingredients, the less processed the food product and the more likely to be healthful and a good food choice.

If you keep the label items and Label Targets in mind the next time you enter your local supermarket, you should arrive at the checkout counter with a majority of low-fat food selections. Your IDEAL Eating Plan will have already begun. And with your Fat Counter in hand when dining—whether at home or in your favorite restaurant—you can eat the IDEAL way anywhere, anytime.

The next chapter will help you to slash fat even more by showing you how to cut the fat in recipes while boosting the nutritional value—and the taste.

10

IDEAL Food Preparation: Recipe Streamlining

A few years ago, my idea of making a home-cooked meal for myself was limited to a juicy steak into the broiler or barbecuing burgers and hot dogs. As I gradually altered my eating habits, however, I began to seek out easy recipes and short-cuts for preparing low-fat meals at home. And you know what? It's not nearly as difficult as I had once imagined. In fact, preparing meals the IDEAL way can be simple, fast, and fun! And the results are delicious as well as nutritious, low in fat, and a helpful boon to weight-loss efforts. Cooking for yourself provides *an added sense of control* over your food intake—and over your food budget as well.

Lean Buys

Some wise buys to help you prepare low-fat meals include:

- Nonstick cookware—investing in several pots and pans coated with Silverstone can save immensely on added fat in cooking.
- Blender or food processor—great for making low-fat yogurt

drinks, low-fat dressings, mock sour cream (see recipe on page 188), and other ideal lowfat recipes.

- Wok—stir-fried vegetable dishes prepared with small amounts (¼ to ½ teaspoon per serving) of olive or peanut oil are almost limitless in variety and real easy to create.
- Bulb baster—useful in removing fat from sauces and gravies.
- Gravy separator—used to drain the nonfat juices from meat drippings.
- Pastry brush—used to spread oil *lightly* when greasing pans, in order to carefully control added fat.
- Steamer—for steaming vegetables to make easy, quick, nutrient-rich, tasty dishes.
- Poultry shears and extra sharp knives—useful in removing poultry skin and trimming meat fat as closely as possible.
- Microwave oven—it *is* faster, and it reduces vitamin losses.

COOK CREATIVELY

The key to cooking the IDEAL way is to keep fats to a minimum while creating nutritious and highly palatable products. With fruits and vegetables, *keep it simple:* The less you do to produce, the better it will be for you. Since nutrients and fiber nestle in or just under the skin, avoid scraping and peeling produce if you can. Wash well, pat dry with paper toweling, and serve raw lightly steamed, baked, or poached in juice or dry wine. Purée fruits to serve as sauces for other fruits, or top with a dollop of plain low-fat yogurt (or try the vanilla or lemon flavors for added sweetness). Frozen vegetables are often a better nutritional bargain, as fresh produce can lose significant amounts of vitamin C during storage. Skip the seasoned/sauced vegetables in favor of a sprinkle of pepper and a squeeze of fresh lemon. A *light* dusting of grated Parmesan cheese adds minimal fat and zips up the flavor.

Ever try bulgur wheat in place of your standard mashed potatoes? Kasha instead of white rice? Millet to replace bread stuffing? A tabbouleh salad? These grains are now sold in many supermarkets and can be found in most health food stores. Be creative and be daring: Try cooking with some whole grains you may never have tasted (or heard of) before:

- Bulgur—precooked whole-wheat berries
- Kasha—roasted buckwheat kernels
- Millet—a whole grain used as a side dish or to replace bread in stuffings
- Tabbouleh—cracked wheat salad, served cold with tomato and mint
- Couscous—cracked wheat berries, served with vegetables or fruit
- Amaranth—a South American whole grain used as a side dish or in cereal
- Quinoa (pronounced KEEN-wa)—a South American whole-grain flour
- Triticale—a hybrid of wheat and rye, with over 25 percent more protein than whole wheat

I'm not going to advocate that you should make all your own breads from scratch. Most of us don't have the time for such industrious home baking. But you might want to experiment with bread baking once in a while. There's nothing like the aroma of freshly baked bread, and since you can reduce the fat to a minimal amount in most bread recipes (and eliminate it altogether in soda bread), generous servings of your whole-grain loaves and rolls are allowable. With quick breads, muffins, pancakes, and waffles, you can alter standard recipes to reduce fat and increase nutritional value. Substitute vegetable oil for butter in recipes (use ¾ tablespoon oil for each tablespoon of butter), and then try cutting the vegetable oil from as much as ¼ cup to a single tablespoon. The recipe should still yield a tasty product, but with a lot less (saturated and total) fat. By substituting whole-grain flour for half of the white flour in recipes, you can add nutrients, fiber, and a heartier flavor. Try my favorite oat bran muffin recipe (see pages 143–144) to see just how tasty low-fat nutrition can be.

In preparing desserts, cut down the quantities of high-fat ingredients. Substitute vegetable oil for butter, and reduce the amount called for by the recipe. You can also cut the sugar, by as much as one-quarter to one-half, and still achieve sweet (but not *too* sweet) results. Cocoa powder is a reduced-fat substitute for chocolate (3 tablespoons cocoa powder plus 1 teaspoon vegetable oil = 1 square of baker's chocolate). Some people like the "chocolaty" flavor of carob. Commercial desserts containing carob, however, usually have added fat for flavor.

Since you need *more than twice as many servings* from the fruit and vegetable food group and from the bread and cereals food group as you do from the meat and meat alternates group, cook your meals accordingly. Instead of roasts or chops, experiment with stir-fry vegetable dishes merely flavored with *small amounts* of skinless chicken or lean beef. Try vegetable casseroles with rice or barley and a little lean lamb or veal for flavor. What about whole-wheat pastas with scallops or clams? Delicious!

When you want to serve meat, poultry, or fish as the main dish, be sure to choose lean cuts. Trim off the skin and any visible fat, and cook without added fats. Some beef is now labeled with the percentage of fat, so you can look for "extra lean" (may be less than 5 percent fat) cuts. The "standard" and the "select" grades of meat have less fat than "choice" (5 to 20 percent more fat) or "prime" (with over 40 percent more fat). When baking, broiling, or roasting lean cuts, reduce the cooking time or the meat will toughen up. Be sure to drain off fats *during* as well as after cooking. Grilling allows some of the fat to drip out, but studies indicate that cancer-causing chemicals are formed during the process. (So much for my grilled burgers!) Hamburger meat is highly fatty anyway. Ask the meat department butcher to grind up well-trimmed sirloin, top round, or chuck beef, then use it sparingly as a flavor enhancer, as in casseroles.

Spray oils (Pam, etc.) are handy for those of us who hate scrubbing pots and pans, but I would rather use a small amount of vegetable oil (¼ teaspoon = 10 fat calories). Why? Because spray oils *are* oil (corn or soybean), and at a gram of fat per teaspoon, a heavy spray can contribute a considerable amount of fat. Moreover, these products contain a host of chemical additives, preservatives, and propellants. Not that such additives have all proven to be unsafe in the amounts we generally consume, but I nevertheless prefer to limit my intake of unnecessary additives. I don't like the aroma of spray oils anyway!

Liquid vegetable oils, on the other hand, *can* be used in cooking—*in small amounts*. As you remember from chapter 8, the best choices for health reasons are the less saturated oils:

- Safflower
- Sesame
- Sunflower
- Cottonseed
- Corn
- Rapeseed (canola)
- Soybean
- Olive
- Peanut

If you use margarine, the squeeze bottles and soft tubs with a liquid vegetable oil listed as the first (that is, primary) ingredient are the least saturated choices. As far as weight and fat control are concerned, however, *fat is fat* and they're all equally fattening. So when you do cook with fats, be very frugal in your use of vegetable oils and margarine or butter. This goes for all of the other sources of food fat as well, such as cream, sour cream, and nuts.

STREAMLINE YOUR CHEESE CHOICES

A sneaky source of hidden fat in many delicious dishes is cheese. In cooking, low-fat cottage cheese and part-skim ricotta are excellent substitutes for higher-fat cheeses, especially in casserole dishes. A *light* sprinkling of Parmesan can go a long way as flavoring—use it sparingly in place of grated high-fat cheeses. Be aware that some part-skim cheeses and certain so-called "low-fat" brands are actually not all that low in total fat. Cheeses labeled "low cholesterol" are often high in *fat*, with vegetable oil replacing the milk fat in equivalent amounts. The following lists can help you in the selection of *lower*-fat cheeses.

FAT IN CHEESES

LOW-FAT CHEESES (less than 3 grams per ounce):

- Cottage cheese, low-fat (2%)
- Light cream cheese
- Light Line low-fat cheese
- Part-skim ricotta
- Skim milk farmer's cheese
- Weight Watchers low-fat cheese
- Yogurt cheese

MEDIUM-FAT CHEESES (4–6 grams per ounce):

- Cheezola
- Creamed cottage cheese (4.2% milk fat)
- Feta
- Whole milk mozzarella
- Part-skim mozzarella
- Parmesan
- Ricotta
- Sapsago
- Most so-called low-fat cheeses (except the brands listed above and others specifically labeled to indicate 3 grams fat per ounce or less)

HIGH-FAT CHEESES (more than 7 grams per ounce):

- American
- Blue
- Brick
- Brie, camembert
- Cheddar
- Cheese foods
- Cheese spreads
- Colby
- Cream cheese
- Edam, Gouda
- Fontina
- Mini-chol
- Muenster, jack
- Neufchâtel
- Provalone
- Romano
- Roquefort
- Swiss, gruyère
- Jarlsburg

CHEESE SERVING SIZES

1 oz. cottage or ricotta cheese = 2 Tbsp.

1 oz. cream cheese = 2 Tbsp.

1 oz. yogurt cheese = 2 Tbsp.

1 oz. grated cheese = ⅓ cup

1 oz. hard and semisoft cheeses = 1½-inch cube or
   3½ × 3½ × ⅛-inch slice

KITCHEN EXPERIMENTS

Whole-milk products can add significant amounts of fat when used in recipes, so it is a good idea to substitute the low-fat, nonfat, and skim milk forms. To thicken up skim milk, stir in some nonfat powdered milk. Dried skim milk powder can also be used to thicken sauces. Instead of fat, you'll be adding protein and calcium to your recipes! Try powdered skim milk to lighten your coffee; it's a good replacement for those fatty creamers.

Use the following tip sheets for lowering the fat in recipes and to help you in making your cooking creations as IDEAL as possible.

A Baker's Dozen Tips for Lowering Fat

1. Use nonstick pans.
2. Steam, poach, bake, roast, broil, and boil without adding fats.
3. Sauté in broth and/or dry wine instead of oil and/or butter.
4. Buy lean meats, trim well before cooking, and remove all noticeable fat before serving.
5. Use standard and select cuts instead of prime and choice meats.
6. Remove skin from poultry before cooking.
7. Use meats in small amounts to *complement* vegetable and/or grain dishes.

188 • *The IDEAL Weight Loss Program*

8. Chill broths and soups (including canned soups) and skim off all congealed fat.
9. Use nonfat powdered milk or puréed vegetables to thicken sauce.
10. Use a *light* sprinkling of Parmesan cheese or true low-fat cheese choices to replace whole-milk cheeses.
11. Use skim milk in place of whole milk or cream (add some nonfat milk powder to thicken), and use low-fat yogurt in place of sour cream or mayonnaise.
12. Use liquid or soft margarine, diet margarine, imitation/diet mayonnaise, low-fat yogurt, MOCK SOUR CREAM, and YOGURT CHEESE for lower-fat spreads.
13. Use your imagination to create new recipes low in fat but high in taste appeal.

MOCK SOUR CREAM

- Blend 1 cup low-fat cottage cheese with 3 tablespoons butter-milk and 1 to 2 teaspoons lemon juice until smooth and tasty.

or

- Blend 2 cups low-fat cottage cheese with 1/2 cup low-fat yogurt and 2 to 3 teaspoons lemon juice until smooth and tasty.

YOGURT CHEESE

Use as a spread, a low-fat substitute for butter, margarine, cream cheese, and sour cream. Mix with a little mayonnaise to pick up the flavor of sandwiches and sandwich fillings.

- Line a strainer with a paper coffee filter and place over a bowl.
- Pour in plain low-fat yogurt.
- Let drain overnight, uncovered, in the refrigerator.
- Scoop out yogurt cheese from the strainer, and discard "whey" in bowl.

A Baker's Dozen Tips for Enhancing Nutrient Value

1. Wash produce quickly and avoid soaking.
2. Peel fruits and vegetables only when necessary, and scrape *lightly* if required.
3. Steam vegetables if possible. If boiling, reserve liquid for use in stocks, soups, and stews.
4. Vary salad greens with romaine and bibb lettuce, escarole and chicory, spinach and kale, watercress and endive, other nutritious greens.
5. Make your own baked goods and desserts to monitor fat and control other ingredients.
6. Use one-half whole-grain flour in place of white flour in breads and rolls, quick breads and muffins, cookies and crackers, pancakes and waffles.
7. Use wheat germ, unprocessed bran, rolled oats, and whole cornmeal in baked goods.
8. Reduce sugar called for in recipes by one-quarter or more.
9. Sweeten homemade desserts with fruit juice or puréed fruit.
10. Flavor foods with herbs and spices instead of salt and high-sodium seasonings.
11. Buy low-sodium condiments and salad dressings.
12. In recipes with eggs, use two whites to replace one whole egg, or two whites plus one whole egg to replace two whole eggs.
13. Be willing to experiment and to practice with new recipes and revisions for old favorites.

Cookbook Selection Checklist

Before you purchase that new "low-fat" cookbook with the oh-so-attractive cover, check carefully to see that the contents live up to your expectations:

- Are the recipes clear, easy to understand, doable?
- Are the ingredients familiar, readily available, affordable?

- Do the recipe yields suit your personal needs?
- Do the recipes appeal to you?
- Does each recipe include a nutritional analysis with the fat (in grams) per serving?
- Are the fat contents for most recipes less than 4 grams per serving?
- Do the recipes substitute low-fat ingredients for the high-fat items (for example, low-fat yogurt for sour cream, low-fat milk for whole milk and cream)?
- Is vegetable oil used in place of butter?
- Do many of the recipes use meats as a condiment instead of as the main ingredient?
- Do the recipes use cheese judiciously? Eggs? Nuts? Convenience foods? Imitation products?
- Are the recipes low in cholesterol? High in fiber? Low in sodium? (Check the nutritional analyses.)
- Are the desserts rich (that is, high in fat and/or sugar)?
- Will you need to make major recipe adjustments to create low-fat dishes from this cookbook? In other words, is it really worth buying?

DO UNTO OTHERS

"I'd *like* to change my eating habits, but I have a spouse and/or children to feed. *They* certainly won't want to eat what *I'm* going to be eating." If these concerns are holding you back from making a commitment to dietary change, I have good news for you. The IDEAL Eating Plan will not only put *your* weight under control, but it is designed to meet your family's nutritional requirements and contribute to their good health as well. Except for children under the age of two, a well-balanced *low-fat* diet is the ideal way to eat.

For women in particular, nurturing the family often takes precedence over nurturing themselves. But by improving your own state of physical well-being, you can serve as a valuable role model for your family. When you feel healthy, fit, and in control, you'll inspire your family to follow suit—and you'll probably be a lot happier and more fun to live with! In the next chapter, I will provide some special dietary considerations just for women.

IDEAL Living

CHAPTER

11

For Females Only: What Women Must Know About the Nutrients They Need

Women generally have lower caloric requirements than men but need most nutrients in equivalent or *greater* amounts. To make matters more trying, women's nutritional needs change markedly through the life cycle, with pregnancy as one obvious reason. The monthly cycles of menstruation also can affect nutrient and food intakes. And for the millions of American women struggling to lose or control body weight, there exists this troubling nutritional paradox: How can they successfully obtain more nutrients from less food?

The answer to the puzzle is not to eat less, *but to eat more— more wisely.* With an increase in activity, there is an accompanying increase in your caloric leeway, making it easier to obtain needed nutrients. And when your metabolic rate is permanently stoked, you can really liberalize caloric intakes, ensuring optimal nutrition with room left over for occasional splurges *without weight gain.* This principle works for men, too. But for females, a program of regular exercise can mean the difference between enduring a life-long prison of futile self-starvation and enjoying the liberation of a well-balanced diet.

On this program, you will become truly active, if not downright athletic. The IDEAL Eating Plan will guide you in meeting your nutritional needs without restricting or even tabulating your caloric intakes. So the paradox will be overcome because you'll be able to obtain adequate nutrients from enough food. You'll eat more, yet weigh less—more food and more nutrients, but less fat, making for less body fat.

NUTRITION AND SEX

Since women have special nutritional requirements and dietary needs that fluctuate monthly and throughout their lifetimes, I believe that every woman should take the time to identify all of the potential deficiencies and to recognize her individual cycles. This chapter provides the scientific facts about women's special nutrient requirements, practical dietary guidance for meeting these needs, and the motivation essential for making the necessary changes. This is a special chapter because *you* have special dietary needs.

Women are more prone to nutrient deficiencies—specifically *iron, calcium, folic acid,* and *vitamin B_6*. Does this mean you should rely on vitamin and mineral supplements to meet your needs? Not necessarily. Women also gain weight more easily than men. Does this mean you should cut calories to the bone and try to obtain your needed nutrients in pill form? Definitely not. Let your female sex work for you instead of against you. Nurture yourself wisely and well, for the sake of your good health, good looks, and good sense.

As you may have guessed, the first step I suggest is a thorough self-evaluation. Take out your IDEAL Log and record your answers to the self-evaluation below to determine your current know-how about a woman's nutritional and dietary needs.

Self-Evaluation: Nutrition for Women

1. Which of these foods are high in iron?

Hummus	Blackstrap	Wild rice
Steamed clams	molasses	Fortified ready-to-
Dried peaches	Oysters	eat cereals
	Lima beans	Eggs

2. Which of these foodstuffs are high in vitamin C?

Black currants	Cauliflower	Broccoli
Strawberries	Tomatoes	Fortified ready-to-
Chili peppers	Lemon juice	eat cereals
		Apple juice

3. True or false? Prolonged fatigue is a sure sign of iron deficiency anemia.
4. True or false? The average American diet includes 10 milligrams of iron per 1000 calories.
5. True or false? Use of cast iron cookware is no longer recommended because iron will leach into cooking foodstuffs to ruin food flavor.
6. Which of these foodstuffs are high in calcium?

Skim milk	Steamed broccoli	Low-lactose milk
Blackstrap	Nonfat vanilla	Sour cream
molasses	yogurt	Eggs
Canned	Tofu	
salmon		

7. Which of the foodstuffs in the list above are high in fat?
8. True or false? It is difficult for women to include adequate calcium in the daily diet without consuming excessive fat calories.
9. True or false? The calcium in milk products is more readily absorbed by the body than from most other sources, including supplements.

10. Which of these foodstuffs are good sources of vitamin B$_6$?

Baked potato	Spinach	Orange juice
Bananas	Avocado	Fortified ready-to-
Oatmeal	Liver	eat cereals
		Eggs

11. Which of the foodstuffs in the list above are good sources of folic acid?
12. True or false? Long-term use of oral contraceptives can result in nutritional imbalances.
13. True or false? Supplementation with the water-soluble vitamin B$_6$ can be regarded as risk-free.
14. True or false? Premenstrual syndrome (PMS) is a psychological disorder with physical symptoms but without physiological basis.
15. Which of the following supplements have proven effective in treating PMS?

Vitamin B$_6$	Evening primrose oil
Vitamin E	Multivitamins in megadoses
Magnesium	Caffeine-containing diuretics

16. True or false? Premenstrual cravings for carbohydrate-rich foods are best ignored.
17. True or false? Supplemental use of vitamin E can be regarded as risk-free.
18. True or false? Overweight women should gain at least fifteen pounds during pregnancy.
19. True or false? The choice not to breastfeed is the major contributing factor to postpregnancy obesity.
20. True or false? The postpregnancy period is an ineffectual time for a new mother to attempt to boost her body's nutrient (especially calcium and iron) stores.
21. Which of these lifestyle factors can contribute to accelerated bone loss?

| High-protein diet | Coffee consumption | Inactivity |
| | | Low-calorie dieting |

| Soft drink consump-tion | Cigarette smoking | Aging |
| Diet soft drink consump-tion | Alcohol intake | |

22. True or false? Bone loss is a natural process of aging that begins around the age of fifty.
23. True or false? The risk for breast cancer may be reduced with specific dietary alterations.
24. True or false? A low carbohydrate and/or restricted caloric intake often triggers physiologically driven eating binges.
25. True or false? It is more difficult for women to maintain a healthy weight than it is for their male peers.

Answers to Self-Evaluation:

1. All provide significant amounts of iron except eggs (which contain an iron-binding factor that blocks absorption of the available iron).
2. All provide ample amounts of vitamin C except for cereals and apple juice that have *not* been fortified with this nutrient.
3. False, not in all cases.
4. False. It's more like 6 milligrams per 1000 calories.
5. False.
6. All provide good amounts of calcium except for sour cream and eggs.
7. Sour cream is high in fat; eggs are relatively high in fat; low-lactose *whole* milk is high in fat; tofu contains some fat, as does salmon, but these sources are highly unsaturated.
8. False.
9. True.
10. Baked potato, bananas, oatmeal, spinach, avocado, and liver are good sources of vitamin B_6; cereals fortified with 100 percent of the U.S. RDA for this vitamin can also serve as a useful source.
11. Spinach, avocado, liver, and orange juice are good sources of

folic acid; cereals fortified with 100 percent of the U.S. RDA for this B vitamin can also serve as a useful source.

12. True.
13. False, and megadoses can prove toxic.
14. False. There is indeed a physiological basis for PMS.
15. None has been proven effective, and caffeine can aggravate symptoms.
16. False.
17. False.
18. True.
19. True.
20. False. This is in fact an excellent time to boost nutrient stores.
21. All can contribute to the development of osteoporosis, the bone-thinning disorder commonly associated with aging.
22. False, bone loss accelerates significantly after menopause but begins during the *third* decade of life.
23. True.
24. True, and such binges are not only due to psychological deprivation but to inner biological drives.
25. True, but it *can* be done!

UPPING IRON INTAKES

An essential mineral, iron is an integral component of hemoglobin, the pigment in red blood cells that carries oxygen to all of your body's tissues. Inadequate iron results in an energy crisis and directly affects the brain and nervous system. Even slightly lowered iron levels, which can occur long before the all-out deficiency stage known as anemia, can cause changes in behavior, mood, and attention span. If you are iron deficient, you will suffer from fatigue, weakness, paleness, and irritability.

Unfortunately, 10 to 20 percent of American women of childbearing age have some form of iron deficiency. Your iron stores are apt to be unhealthfully low if you fit into one or more of the following categories:

- Teenage girls—and still growing
- Pregnant women or those in the first two to three months following delivery

- Endurance athletes, especially runners
- Vegetarians and red meat eschewers
- Dieters—chronic low-calorie eaters

All women are susceptible to a deficiency in iron *at least* one time during their lives. Since the average diet includes only 6 milligrams of iron for every 1000 calories, most women fail to meet their daily requirement of 18 milligrams.

The IDEAL Eating Plan can help you to obtain adequate iron while you are losing weight. The key is to eat adequate amounts of foods high in iron but to limit your fat intake. Use the "High in Iron" food list that follows to help you make iron-rich menu selections. Note that the "heme" iron sources (that is, animal products) are better absorbed by the body than "nonheme" iron (from nonanimal sources, including iron supplements). *You can significantly enhance the nonheme iron absorption from foods by combining with heme iron sources and/or foodstuffs rich in vitamin C.*

HIGH IN IRON

Heme Sources
MEATS AND SEAFOOD:

Beef liver	Shrimp
Clams	Sardines
Oysters	Chicken or turkey—dark meat
Lean beef	Lean lamb
Lean veal	Tuna and other dark fish

Nonheme Sources
MEAT ALTERNATES:

Baked beans	Kidney beans
Lima beans	Lentils
Garbanzo beans (chickpeas)	Peas
Hummus	Tofu
Navy beans	

FRUITS AND VEGETABLES:

Dried peaches	Swiss chard
Dried apricots	Mustard greens
Raisins	Dandelion greens
Dried figs	Kale
Dates	Turnip greens
Prunes	Broccoli
Prune juice	Baked potato
Spinach	Sweet potato
Beet greens	

BREADS AND CEREALS:

Ready-to-eat cereal, enriched or fortified	Brown rice
Whole-grain cereal	Whole-grain bread
Wild rice	Enriched bread
Enriched rice	Bran muffins

EXTRAS:

Blackstrap molasses

HIGH IN VITAMIN C
These foods aid iron absorption.

FRUITS:

Black currants	Lemons
Cantaloupe	Limes
Citrus juices	Mangos
Grapefruit	Oranges
Guava	Papaya
Kiwi	Strawberries

VEGETABLES:

Broccoli	Sweet peppers
Brussels sprouts	Chili peppers
Cauliflower	Tomatoes
Collard greens	Tomato juice
Kale	Turnip greens
Mustard greens	

How do these iron-rich menus sound to you?

- Breakfast—fortified wheat cereal with raisins and dates, skim milk, fresh orange juice
- Lunch— whole-grain spaghetti with clams and tomato sauce
- Dinner— stir-fried tofu and vegetables, complemented with lean beef strips and slivered almonds
- Snack— whole-grain crackers with hummus, raisin and peanut mix, low-fat strawberry yogurt drink

By using iron-rich red meat as a flavor enhancer, not a main dish, you can add significant amounts of iron to your weekly diet without sabotaging your low-fat eating patterns. And by supplementing dried beans and peas, dried fruits, green vegetables, and cereals with good sources of vitamin C, you can meet your iron needs while controlling your weight. See the iron-rich cooking tips below for additional ideas on upping your iron intakes.

Iron-Rich Cooking Tips

- Use of cast iron cookware can enhance the iron content of home-cooked meals by leaching the mineral from pots and pans into the cooking foodstuffs (flavor is unaffected).
- Prepare tomato sauces in cast iron skillets, and let simmer for extended periods to increase iron content significantly.
- Add blackstrap molasses to recipes for baked goods to serve as all or part of the sweetener.

- Use blackstrap molasses to sweeten milk drinks and yogurt (for example, molasses-flavored low-fat milkshakes and low-fat yogurt shakes).
- Tannins, chemicals naturally present in tea and carob, block iron absorption; so does coffee, but to a lesser extent. Use sparingly.

Important note: If you are constantly fatigued, weak, listless, and pale, see your physician. These symptoms could be indicative of anemia, which may or may not be due to iron deficiency and might require prescribed supplementation. Such symptoms can also be caused by other serious health conditions requiring medical attention.

COUNT ON CALCIUM

A common myth is that our bones are inert substances, that calcium is stored there forever like the minerals in a rock. Unfortunately for us, this is not true. Our bones are in a constant state of flux, and the calcium losses eventually exceed absorption as an inevitable process of aging. While we are children, teenagers, and young adults, we can still store up calcium and build up strong bones. But sometime in the midst of the third decade, the body's balance shifts. And after age fifty, the rate of bone loss is significantly increased in women.

Women tend to have lighter bones, so have less calcium to lose before problems begin to occur. Osteoporosis, adult bone loss with the resulting ease of fracture and loss of height from spinal bone abnormalities, is ten times more common in females. Millions of American women who develop this debilitating disease have one major lifestyle factor in common: They fail to obtain adequate dietary calcium.

Many women cut back on or cut out milk sometime during the teen years, often to save on calories. This is when the problem takes root, at a time when bones are still capable of storing up calcium as protection against the forthcoming losses. The long-term results of low calcium intakes are devastating, even fatal. Some forty thousand American women *die* every year due to pneumonia, blood clots, and other serious complications that develop during the prolonged immobility of osteoporosis. Is it worth it, saving those few calories? Certainly not. And with the array of low-fat choices available, avoiding milk products is unnecessary for weight watchers anyway.

Around 80 percent of the world's population is affected by an inherited condition known as "lactose intolerance." If the enzyme needed during the digestion of milk sugar (lactose) is inadequate or ineffective, unpleasant gastrointestinal side effects occur whenever milk is consumed. Many lactose intolerant people can tolerate *small amounts* of milk, especially when consumed with a meal. Most can eat yogurt and cheese without experiencing gastric upset. If you think that you may be lactose intolerant, test out your individual tolerances before you totally eliminate all calcium-rich milk products from your daily diet. Try drinking milk products with reduced lactose content. And consult your physician about your suspicions.

Nonmilk sources of calcium are not as readily absorbed by the body, primarily because lactose seems to act as an absorption enhancer. Vitamin D also helps the body to absorb calcium, and milk is fortified with this essential vitamin. But the contributions of other high-calcium foodstuffs can certainly add up, improving total intakes and adding to the body's stores. Use the "High in Calcium" list that follows to make your food choices count.

HIGH IN CALCIUM

MILK AND CHEESE:

Low-fat yogurt
Parmesan cheese
Part-skim ricotta
Skim milk
Low-fat milk
Kefir

Soft serve ice milk
Low-fat frozen yogurt
Low-fat cottage cheese
Low-fat cheeses
Nonfat dried milk powder

VEGETABLES:

Bok choy	Mustard greens
Kale	Broccoli
Turnip greens	

MEAT AND MEAT ALTERNATES:

Sardines (with bones)	Scallops
Mackerel (canned)	Oysters
Salmon (with bones)	Mussels
Herring (canned)	Soybeans
Shrimp	Tofu

EXTRAS:

Custard	Sherbet
Pudding	Pizza
Ice cream	Almonds
Blackstrap molasses	Filberts

The current dietary calcium recommendations of most nutrition experts are for:

- 1000 milligrams per day for teens and adult women of child-bearing age
- 1500 milligrams for postmenopausal women
- 800 milligrams for children and adult males

The typical American woman only takes in around 600 milligrams of calcium per day—or less. Women usually avoid milk and deprive themselves of needed calcium solely because they are dieting. Yet you can obtain adequate amounts of calcium and still lose weight. The key is to eat low-fat high-calcium foods. And regular exercise, such as PaceWalking, can help to build bone strength, too. On this program you can count on good nutrition—including bone-building calcium—and healthful exercise for a strong, healthy, fit (not fat) lifetime.

The list below illustrates dietary factors that can hinder calcium absorption when included in the diet in large quantities. Be wary of *calcium blockers and robbers.* Too much caffeine, protein, or phosphates in the diet can reduce your bones' calcium stores. The oxalates and phytates (found in high-fiber foods and leafy green vegetables) bind up the calcium in these foods during digestion, so are not good sources of this mineral. However, eating these foods will not deplete your body's calcium stores. Just be sure that you are moderate in your intake of the common food sources of calcium blockers and robbers, and avoid low-calorie diets and inactivity in favor of the bone-building IDEAL program.

CALCIUM BLOCKERS AND ROBBERS

Calcium Blockers	Food Sources—Don't Overdo
Oxalates	Rhubarb, spinach, chard, some greens
Phytates	Oat bran, wheat bran, high-fiber cereals
Phosphates	Red meats, soft drinks, processed foods (check labels for phosphate additives)
Caffeine	Coffee, tea, cola drinks, chocolate

Calcium Robbers	Common Causes—Avoid if Possible
High protein intakes	Protein supplements, diets high in meat and animal products
Inactivity	Illness, sedentary lifestyle
Low-calorie diets	Fad diets, chronic low-calorie dieting

DON'T BYPASS THE B's

Surveys of the typical dietary intakes of today's female population indicate that more than one-third of American women are deficient in one *or more* nutrients. Two of the B vitamins in particular, folic acid and B_6, are most commonly deficient. Folic acid is essential for proper blood cell formation, and vitamin B_6 has many important functions in the body, including maintenance of healthy skin and nerves. A deficiency in folic acid leads to the weakness, fatigue, and the lethargy of folacin-deficiency anemia. Inadequate B_6 intakes can cause a variety of side effects, *most notably depression*. For many women, deficiencies in one or both of these vitamins go undiagnosed and untreated.

Pregnancy significantly elevates the need for folic acid, while use of oral contraceptives tends to decrease blood levels of this B vitamin. Does this necessitate a reliance on folic acid supplements? Fortunately, your diet can supply you with ample amounts of this important nutrient if foods rich in folic acid—such as orange juice, fortified breakfast cereals, and leafy green vegetables—are consumed regularly. You can use the "High in Folic Acid" list below to note these and other good food sources of this B vitamin. Note also that most folic acid–rich foods are naturally low in fat content.

HIGH IN FOLIC ACID

Liver	Greens—beet, mustard, turnip
Orange juice	Spinach
Fortified ready-to-eat cereals	Lima beans
Wheat germ	Navy beans
Asparagus	Peanuts
Broccoli	Almonds
Brussels sprouts	Avocado

Oral contraceptive use can lead to nutritional imbalances, including vitamin B_6 deficiency. This is believed to be one reason why many users suffer from depression. Pregnancy elevates the need for vitamin B_6, as does alcohol intake. Supplementation is usually unnecessary, however, when dietary sources of B_6—such as bananas, lean meats, poultry, fish, and potatoes—are included regularly. You can use the "High in Vitamin B_6" list that follows to note these and other good food sources of this essential nutrient, most of which are low or moderately low in fat content.

HIGH IN VITAMIN B$_6$	
Bananas	Whole-grain cereals
Fortified ready-to-eat cereals	Legumes
Liver	Potato, baked
Lean meats	Spinach
Chicken, turkey	Collard and other greens
Tuna, salmon	Avocado

Be wary of the lure of supplement salesfolk who attempt to convince you that your womanly needs automatically necessitate extra doses of various forms of vitamin B. Excessive vitamin B intakes are not only unnecessary, but with B$_6$ can prove toxic! Megadoses of this vitamin have actually caused serious nerve damage in unsuspecting supplement users.

THOSE PMS BLUES

Do you usually get cranky during the week prior to your period? Do your breasts feel tender, your body bloated? Are you tired, irritable, not at your best just before menstruating every month? If any or all of these symptoms plague you on a monthly basis, you probably suffer from the common disorder known as premenstrual syndrome (PMS). But you don't have to feel all alone in your woes. Up to nine out of ten menstruating women undergo noteworthy psychological and physical changes during the week before their periods. And 10 to 20 percent suffer from symptoms that are severe and serious enough to interfere with their day-to-day lives.

The basis for PMS is hormonal, and the treatment is usually lifestyle change. Studies indicate that women who follow well-balanced diets and exercise regularly have less trouble with PMS than those who maintain less healthful living patterns. This program can help to reduce the symptoms of PMS for those who suffer from:

- Fatigue— eating regular meals and avoiding high sugar intakes can help to even out blood sugar levels,

combatting the low blood sugar associated with PMS.
- Bloating—moderating salt/sodium intake can help reduce water retention in those who are sodium sensitive.
- Breast tenderness—avoiding or minimizing caffeine can help those with breast tissue enzymes overly sensitive to this chemical.
- Moodiness and depression—adequate intakes of carbohydrate and vitamin B$_6$ (from food sources) can reduce hormonally induced mood swings.

Chronic dieting can contribute to PMS symptoms, especially the psychological side effects. It is important for women to understand that *the body's caloric needs change during the monthly cycle.* Your body actually needs more calories during ovulation (mid-cycle) and during the week before you menstruate. This is because your metabolic rate speeds up premenstrually. This can pick up your appetite, which is why food cravings—commonly a desire for carbohydrates—tend to occur during the week before menstruation. Dieters should realize that during the premenstrual period they are struggling against a natural hormone-induced elevation in the body's metabolism. This means *there is a natural increase in appetite for food in general, starches and sweets in particular, and specifically chocolate for some.* Fighting the body's urges often leads to binge eating, depression, and feelings of frustration and guilt.

So what is the best advice for PMS sufferers and weight-watching women with monthly cravings?

- Watch out for too much sugar, salt, and caffeine (see the lists of sugar-rich and sodium-rich, salty foods on pages 145–147 and the "Sources of Caffeine" list below).
- Be sure to obtain adequate vitamins (notably B$_6$—see "High in Vitamin B$_6$" list earlier in this chapter) and other essential nutrients.
- *Don't diet!*

Learn to respect your monthly cycles and to respect your body's wisdom. If you crave sweets premenstrually, indulge with a high-carbohydrate, low-fat snack such as one or two fig bars, a cup of frozen low-fat yogurt, or a *moderate serving* of something chocolate. Instead of ignoring your body's natural demands or overindulging in both fatty foods and guilty feelings, use the IDEAL Eating Plan and the Fat Counter to satisfy your cravings healthfully.

Be wary of supplement salespersons who tout PMS remedies in the form of nutrient pills, such as vitamin B_6 supplements. Two other common PMS "cures"—neither of which has been proven effective—are vitamin E (with or without the "magical" evening primrose oil, extracted from the seeds of the primrose plant) and magnesium. Vitamin E in large doses can cause some unpleasant side effects, including flulike symptoms. Magnesium megadoses can be toxic.

A look at the "High in Vitamin E" and "High in Magnesium" charts below can show you how easy it is to obtain adequate amounts of these two nutrients by eating wisely and eating well.

HIGH IN VITAMIN E

Vegetable oils	Liver
Margarine	Soybeans
Wheat germ oil	Legumes
Olive oil	Nuts
Peanut oil	Olives
Wheat germ	Chocolate(!)
Whole grains	

HIGH IN MAGNESIUM

Oatmeal	Peanuts
Whole grains	Almonds
Wheat germ	Filberts
Black-eyed peas	Brazil nuts
Pinto beans	Pistachios
Soybeans	Cashews
Spinach	Walnuts

If you find that you are sensitive to caffeine at certain times of the month—or any time—you may want to avoid all sources of caffeine, as listed below. A moderate daily intake for people who are not sensitive to caffeine is around 200 milligrams. It is best to avoid potent sources of caffeine, such as alertness tablets and diet pills.

SOURCES OF CAFFEINE

		Mg. Caffeine
COFFEE*		
5-oz. cup:	Brewed, drip method	60–180
	Brewed, percolator	40–170
	Instant	30–120
	Decaffeinated, brewed	2–5
	Decaffeinated, instant	1–5
TEA**		
5-oz. cup:	Brewed, major U.S. brands	20–90
	Brewed, imported brands	25–110
	Instant	25–50
12-oz. glass:	Iced	65–75
COCOA AND CHOCOLATE:		
5-oz. cup:	Cocoa beverage	2–20
8 oz.	Chocolate milk beverage	2–7
1 oz.:	Dark chocolate, semisweet	5–35
	Baking chocolate	25
	Milk chocolate	1–15
	Chocolate syrup	4

*Alternatives to coffee that are 100 percent caffeine-free are the cereal-based beverages Postum, Cafix, and Pero.
**Some herbal teas contain caffeine, others are caffeine-free.

		Mg. Caffeine
SOFT DRINKS:		
12 oz.:	Sugar-Free Mr. Pibb	59
	Mountain Dew	54
	Mellow Yellow	53
	Tab	47
	Coca-Cola	46
	Diet Coke	46
	Shasta Cola	44
	Shasta Diet Cola	44
	Sunkist Orange	42
	Mr. Pibb	41
	Dr. Pepper	40
	Sugar-Free Dr. Pepper	40
	Pepsi Cola	38
	Diet Pepsi, Pepsi Light	36
	Diet Rite Cola	36
	RC Cola	36
	Hires Root Beer	0
	7 Up, Fresca, Sprite	0
	Gingerale	0

Over-the-Counter Medications
(Standard Dose)

ALERTNESS TABLETS:	Vivarin	200
	Caffedrin	200
	NoDoz	100
PAIN RELIEVERS:	Excedrin	65
	Vanquish	33
	Anacin	32
	Extra Strength Anacin	32
	Midol	32
	Aspirin, any brand	0

		Mg. Caffeine
COLD/ALLERGY REMEDIES:	Triaminicin	30
	Coryban-D	30
	Duradyre Forte	30
	Dristan	16
DIURETICS:	Permathene H$_2$Off	200
	Maximum Strength Aqua Ban	200
	Aqua Ban	100
	Pre-Mens Forte	100
DIET PILLS:	Dexatrim	200
	Dexatrim Extra Strength	200
	Dietac	200
	Dex-a-Diet II	200
	Codexin	200
	Prolamine	140
	Maximum Strength Appedrine	100
	Acutrim	0

Adapted from Food and Drug Administration, Food Additive Chemistry Evaluation Branch and National Center for Drugs and Biologies, 1984.

POSTBABY BODY BOOM—OR BOON

Contrary to popular opinion, pregnancy and the months immediately following delivery need not be a time for nutritional losses and permanent weight gain. In fact, this important time in a woman's life can prove to be a period for optimizing nutrient stores and achieving desirable body weight.

During pregnancy, your dietary needs are significantly increased. But your body also becomes more efficient in the absorption of certain nutrients, such as iron and calcium. The pregnant woman who eats well can satisfy the nutritional needs of her unborn child while enhancing her own tissue iron and bone calcium stores *to come away from delivery with a net gain in these two essential nutrients*. Pregnant women should consult a nutritionist or dietitian recommended by their physician to ensure the optimal food intake critical during this time.

During the typical pregnancy, some ten to fifteen pounds of fat are deposited in the mother's fat storage depots (adipose tissue). This serves as the stored form of the 30,000 to 45,000 calories needed for the first two to three months of breastfeeding. And if you opt for bottle feeding instead? Then the stored fat will not be naturally shed during lactation. For this reason alone, postpregnancy weight problems occur far more often in women who do not breastfeed. Repeated pregnancies without lactation can add significantly to fat stores and weight problems.

For women who are unable or choose not to breastfeed, limited weight gain during pregnancy is *not* the solution. In fact, overweight women should gain at least fifteen pounds during pregnancy, and a twenty-pound-plus gain is recommended if you are of normal weight. Failure to gain weight during pregnancy threatens the size, the health, even the life of the unborn baby. However, once the baby is born, eating the IDEAL way can assist nonbreastfeeding mothers to shed the unneeded fat—gradually, safely, and permanently (or at least until the next pregnancy). The new mother who chooses to breastfeed should ask her physician to recommend the optimal diet for breast milk production and quality.

Many women experience food cravings during pregnancy. Such urges are natural and should be satisfied—within reason, of course! If your pregnant body cries out for cheese pizza topped with tuna or for mocha-nut ice cream, remember that this is your time to be self-indulgent. As long as all of your nutrient needs are met, your diet can include the foods you may crave (at all kinds of odd times!) without jeopardizing your nutritional status, your pregnancy, or the health of your unborn baby.

Warning: Studies indicate that total abstinence from alcohol and caffeine is prudent during pregnancy.

THE MATURE WOMAN

There are some specific health problems associated with advanced age, which older women should take into consideration. One is osteoporosis, which afflicts some 20 percent of women over age sixty-five. A high-calcium diet coupled with regular physical activity is essential during a woman's later years. In certain cases, supplemental calcium will be prescribed by your physician. Usually, however, the increase in calcium requirements for older females can be met by the addition of *one or two extra servings* from the milk and cheese food group.

Another diet-related and age-related disease is cancer. Breast and uterine cancers are believed to be influenced by dietary factors, and their incidence increases with advancing age. Although we are unable to halt the aging process, we *can* alter our diets for possible prevention purposes. A high-fat diet is generally believed to be linked to certain cancers, although this theory is still the subject of controversy. Low intakes of food sources of *beta-carotenes* (the pigmented precursor of vitamin A) and *cruciferous vegetables* (those belonging to the cabbage family) have also been linked to an increased incidence of certain cancers, but this again is a controversial subject area. Use of specific nutritional supplements, however, has *not* been proven to be protective against cancer.

The IDEAL Eating Plan is low in fat, which is certainly healthful for the cardiovascular system, if not proven to be cancer preventing. The eating plan includes plenty of fruits and vegetables rich in beta-carotenes (see following list) and the cabbage family, cruciferous vegetables (see list below), all nutritious and relatively fat-free—if not proven cancer preventives. And this eating plan allows you to attain and maintain a healthful body weight, which *has* been shown to help prevent cancer. Overweight women have an increased risk for breast, uterine, and ovarian cancer.

For many women (and men, too), the later years serve as a time of gradual weight gain. This is largely due to sedentary living patterns but can also be caused by inappropriate eating behaviors, including excessive fat intake *and chronic dieting*. This program

RICH IN BETA-CAROTENES

*FRUITS:

Apricots—fresh and dried
Cantaloupe
Mangos
Nectarines

Papaya
Peaches
Persimmon

VEGETABLES:

Broccoli
Cabbage**
Carrots
Chicory
Corn**
Greens—beet, collard,
   dandelion, mustard, turnip
Kale
Parsley
Peas**

Pumpkin
Spinach
Summer squash**
Sweet potato
Swiss chard
Tomatoes, tomato juice
Watercress
Winter squash
Zucchini**

*All offer lower amounts than vegetable sources.
**In lesser amounts.

CRUCIFEROUS VEGETABLES

Broccoli
Brussels sprouts
Cabbage (coleslaw, sauerkraut)

Cauliflower
Kohlrabi

can prove to be a healthy way for you to lead your later years, as well as a successful method for putting a halt to chronic dieting. It's never too late. And there's no better time to begin than right now!

THE IDEAL DIET—NOT FOR WOMEN ONLY

Definite physiological differences between men and women make achieving nutritional balance and maintenance of a desirable body weight a tougher course for females. I know how tough it once was for me to eat nutritiously and to slim down. It would have been hard for me to imagine that the struggle could have been even more difficult! But for all of you women who are chronic dieters, constantly battling with your bodies due to Low-Calorie Overweight, I have both sympathy and good news: You can obtain the nutrients you need for optimal health while you lose that excess body weight. No matter what your gender, the IDEAL Weight-Loss Program can work for you. As my friend Nancy, my secretary, and Virginia's typing pool can attest, the IDEAL program *does* work for women, too.

A low-fat eating plan makes room for plenty of nutritious food while allowing for body fat reduction. A program of regular physical activity significantly elevates your metabolic rate so that you can eat well *and* lose weight. For women in particular, exercise can actually mean the difference between a frustrating life of self-starvation and the freedom to eat wisely and enjoyably. By building muscle and boosting metabolism, you can overcome the gender bias to increase your caloric needs. And by eating the low-fat way, you can guard your health while shedding excess poundage—for life.

CHAPTER

12

Fat Control for Life!

"If you treat man as he appears to be, you make him worse than he is. But if you treat man as if he already were what he potentially could be, you make him what he should be."

—Goethe

(This goes for women and children, too!)

I decided to enter my second Ironman distance triathlon in the spring of 1988. I chose the same race I had completed in 1984, the Bud Light Endurance Triathlon, which begins with a 2.4-mile swim in the waters off Cape Cod, followed by a 112-mile bicycle ride across back roads and highways, and ending with a full 26.2-mile marathon run. But this time, I planned to PaceWalk the entire marathon course. And this time, I knew without a doubt that I could do it, that I would meet my personal goals for each leg of the race, that I was going to finish this Ironman in "record" (my own, that is) time.

By accepting and internalizing the belief that I would reach my goals, I was able to make it my reality. If you believe that you are getting stronger and more fit, building muscle and shedding fat, progressing on the program, then you will. *We can become what we believe we will become*. This is a vital concept to understand if you are about to challenge yourself, to try something new and/or change an old behavior. The key is to *begin to believe now* that you can eat well, exercise regularly, and get in shape. And so you will. Your actions and habits will reinforce your beliefs, until healthy living becomes your reality. Believe me, it works.

By now, you *know* the four steps to making lifestyle change:

1. Self-evaluate.
2. Set goals.
3. Plan it.
4. Do it!

So by now, the question to ask yourself is this: *Do you now PRACTICE what you know? Now is the time* to put together all of the information provided in the previous chapters, to create an individualized program that you can readily adopt and follow—and *enjoy* for life.

I truly believe that IDEAL living—healthy eating and regular exercise—can be a natural state of being for all of us. We are all capable of undoing past years of unhealthy conditioning by making gradual changes in diet and activity patterns, marking *just the beginning* of transformation in our lives.

IDEAL living does not mean perfection, but balance. IDEAL living means practicing moderate, nutritious, and pleasurable eating patterns. IDEAL living means exercising regularly and liking it. IDEAL living means feeling fit, healthy, happy with your life and yourself. Probably the best news about IDEAL living is that we can all enjoy it, once we decide that *we deserve to feel great*. I did. Now it's *your* turn!

IN BALANCE

The current fitness boom, which escalated markedly during the 1980s, can contribute to an unbalanced perspective about our physical selves. Despite contemporary stereotypes as to the perfect physique, the IDEAL body is not a perfect body. It is, rather, a healthy and fit body. Physical fitness requires a *balanced* approach to exercise. And to diet.

Now and then, I like to permit myself a splurge, to self-indulge in some of my (former) favorite foods. After completing my first Ironman triathlon, for example, I went to a pancake house, had a huge stack smothered in butter and syrup, with bacon *and* sausage on the side. And when I visit my favorite restaurant, I don't request that they hold the butter. I'm just careful not to overdo. Even self-indulgent splurges can be kept under control.

Practicing healthy eating habits means enjoying food for *psychological satisfaction*—with moderation instead of deprivation.

GOING THROUGH PHASES

When you adopt the IDEAL Eating Plan, be sure to progress through the phases *only when you are ready*. Build changes into your diet slowly, so that your palate and your motivation do not suffer.

A word of warning: Don't let yourself get too carried away with the IDEAL fat goals. If you've been compulsive about calories, it may prove all too easy for you to become obsessed with food fat, perhaps to an unhealthy degree. The fat goals serve as general guidelines, the Fat Counter as a generic guide to assist you in a slow, gradual reduction in dietary fat. As with exercise, I rate fun first with my current attitude toward food, with fitness second and fat loss third. *Moderation is the key* to dietary fat slashing.

STAYING POWER

Unhealthy lifestyle patterns are simply habits, automatic behaviors that are reflexive, almost instantaneous, often mindless. During the winter of 1988, a bad spill on the ski slopes in Vermont left me hobbling around with a fractured kneecap. I couldn't exercise. I could barely walk. This might have proven to be the perfect excuse for me to gain weight, overeating constantly due to depression and self-pity. Believe me, I was tempted to do just that. But instead, I focused my attention on eating nutritious meals to help speed my recovery. Six weeks later, I went skiing in Colorado. And I hadn't gained a pound.

Once you decide to take control, it feels so good that you may be unwilling to stop. This is *staying power*, which can accompany the development of *muscle power*, *mind power*, and *personal power*. Setbacks automatically lead to bouncing back, fleeting failures become lessons from which you learn something about yourself—and then you move on.

MEASURING YOUR PERSONAL SUCCESS

After you have been following the IDEAL program for one month, ask yourself the following questions. Then, in order to evaluate your staying power, your ongoing success on the program, ask yourself these same questions once a month. Each time you do, give yourself the pat on the back that you deserve. Now, doesn't that feel good?

1. *Body weight:* Has your weight dropped? Is it approaching your *healthy weight goal?* (After the first month, weigh yourself once a week at the most. *Body weight does not accurately reflect loss of body fat.*)
2. *Body size measurement:* Has your Waist-Hip Ratio improved? Is it approaching the desirable proportion (of less than 1 for men, less than 0.8 for women)? Are your upper arms and thighs getting more muscular, leaner? How do your clothes fit?
3. *Exercise patterns:* Are you following an exercise plan? Are you exercising regularly and consistently? Are you enjoying it? Can you see an improvement in your fitness level?
4. *Eating patterns:* Are you following a healthy eating plan? Are you eating regular meals—breakfast, lunch, dinner—and well-balanced snacks? Have you curtailed your night eating, binge eating, stress eating, self-starving, and self-stuffing? Is your eating under control? Do you feel physically and emotionally satisfied?
5. *Physical health:* Have you noticed a reduction in the following physical symptoms of Low-Calorie Overweight?

- Dry skin, dry hair
- Intolerance to cold, poor circulation, slow pulse
- Dizziness or lightheadedness (especially on standing)
- Fatigue, lethargy, tiredness after eight hours sleep
- Constipation, bloating, cramps
- Poor sleep, poor memory, inability to concentrate

6. *Psychological health:* Have you noticed a reduction in the following psychological symptoms of Diet-Induced Over-weight?

- Depression
- Moodiness, distractability, irritability
- Compulsion to diet, eating-related guilt
- Anger, frustration, feelings of victimization and outer-imposed control
- Feelings of failure, weakness, susceptibility to temptations
- Overall sense that food or diet dominates your life
- Overall sense that your body/weight problem is responsible for the dissatisfaction in your life

7. *Stress:* Do you feel in control of your life, less victimized and more in charge? Have you noticed a reduction in the following physical symptoms of stress:

- Fatigue
- Headache
- Muscle tension (jaws, neck, lower back)
- Heart palpitations
- Indigestion
- Nausea

Have you noticed a reduction in the following psychological symptoms of stress?

- Depression
- Anxiety
- Quick to anger
- Risk taking
- Alcohol/drug abuse
- Eating binges

Are you actively utilizing stress-reduction methods (exercise or meditation, for example)? Do you feel less threatened by change, more tolerant of life's uncertainties?

8. *Lifestyle patterns:* Have you made any significant changes in behaviors other than your eating and exercise patterns? Are you drinking less alcohol? Are you consuming less caffeine? Have you cut back on or stopped smoking cigarettes? Has your use of nonprescription drugs such as aspirin decreased? Are you consuming fewer artificially sweetened soft drinks and diet foodstuffs? Are you watching television less often? Have you improved communication with your mate, family, friends? Have you made new friends, improved your social life and your sex life?

9. *Self-image:* Has your self-image improved? Have you begun to curtail negative self-abusive thoughts, substituting a more positive outlook? Do you feel better about yourself, healthier and more fit? Has your self-confidence improved? Are you experiencing less inner-directed hostility and more emotional stability? Do you like yourself more, believe in your capabilities, trust your abilities, accept yourself as you are?

10. *Inner self:* Are you tapping into your inner feelings, monitoring them and making appropriate behavior adjustments? Do you feel motivated by inner goals? Are you combining honest insight with the courage to act on your desires, in order to work at getting what you really want? Do you feel empowered, in charge, in control?

BODY-MIND FITNESS

One of the most important underlying themes of the New Age and of this book is the interconnectedness of the body and mind. How you feel about yourself, the self-image you maintain, and what you expect from yourself can exert a powerful influence over how you look and what you are able to do. If you *feel* like a big fat failure, you will *look and act* like one, you will *be* overweight and unsuccessful at changing unhealthful lifestyle patterns. But if you *feel* like a fit, powerful success, you will then *look and live* like a healthy person, and you will indeed *be* in great shape—physically and emotionally. Believe me, *believe in yourself* and you can accomplish amazing feats.

Scientists are just beginning to explore the physiological basis for the body-mind connection. But it is a well-accepted fact that your mind maintains a great deal of control over your physical self. For example, we know that *emotionally* stressed individuals are more prone to *physical* illnesses such as ulcers and heart disease, possibly even cancer. This concept illustrates how the mind and emotions are directly linked to the body and to health. Researchers are now delving into how this interaction occurs, investigating the hormones and other chemicals released during emotional upsurges and their physiological pathways in the body and brain. In the years to come, we will surely be incorporating discoveries from the exciting field of "neuropsychoimmunology" into our lives.

In the meantime, it will prove to be highly empowering for you to recognize the control your mind has over your body. *Take control* of your physical self, your diet and exercise habits, your style of living. Use your muscle power, mind power, personal power to shape your body and your life into exactly what you really want to be. If you accept responsibility for yourself and your body, you can then accomplish all of the goals you have set for weight and fat loss, your diet and exercise plans, your body and your life.

To make your path a great deal smoother, I have designed this step-by-step, easy-to-follow, comprehensible, and comprehensive program for making personal changes in the New Age—and for shedding fat. The IDEAL Weight-Loss Program will help you in conducting honest, accurate self-appraisals. The IDEAL program will assist you in setting reasonable, flexible goals for altering your lifestyle patterns and improving your everyday habits. The program will take you by the hand, guiding you in the development of an individualized exercise plan and a personalized eating plan that suit you and are good for you. And the program will provide you with helpful tips for tapping into inner motivation, for taking control of your body and yourself, so that *you can do it*—and keep on doing it, for life!

Appendixes

A. U.S. Recommended Dietary Allowances

RECOMMENDED DAILY DIETARY ALLOWANCES[a]

Age (years)	Weight (kg)	Weight (lb)	Height (cm)	Height (in)	Protein (g)	Fat-soluble vitamins			Water-soluble vitamins							Minerals					
						Vitamin A (µg RE)[b]	Vitamin D (µg)[c]	Vitamin E (mg TE)[d]	Vitamin C (mg)	Thiamin (mg)	Riboflavin (mg)	Niacin (mg NE)[e]	Vitamin B_6 (mg)	Folacin (µg)[f]	Vitamin B_{12} (µg)	Calcium (mg)	Phosphorus (mg)	Magnesium (mg)	Iron (mg)	Zinc (mg)	Iodine (µg)
Infants																					
0.0–0.5	6	13	60	24	kg × 2.2	420	10	3	35	0.3	0.4	6	0.3	30	0.5[g]	360	240	50	10	3	40
0.5–1.0	9	20	71	28	kg × 2.0	400	10	4	35	0.5	0.6	8	0.6	45	1.5	540	360	70	15	5	50
Children																					
1–3	13	29	90	35	23	400	10	5	45	0.7	0.8	9	0.9	100	2.0	800	800	150	15	10	70
4–6	20	44	112	44	30	500	10	6	45	0.9	1.0	11	1.3	200	2.5	800	800	200	10	10	90
7–10	28	62	132	52	34	700	10	7	45	1.2	1.4	16	1.6	300	3.0	800	800	250	10	10	120
Males																					
11–14	45	99	157	62	45	1000	10	8	50	1.4	1.6	18	1.8	400	3.0	1200	1200	350	18	15	150
15–18	66	145	176	69	56	1000	10	10	60	1.4	1.7	18	2.0	400	3.0	1200	1200	400	18	15	150
19–22	70	154	177	70	56	1000	7.5	10	60	1.5	1.7	19	2.2	400	3.0	800	800	350	10	15	150
23–50	70	154	178	70	56	1000	5	10	60	1.4	1.6	18	2.2	400	3.0	800	800	350	10	15	150
51+	70	154	178	70	56	1000	5	10	60	1.2	1.4	16	2.2	400	3.0	800	800	350	10	15	150
Females																					
11–14	46	101	157	62	46	800	10	8	50	1.1	1.3	15	1.8	400	3.0	1200	1200	300	18	15	150
15–18	55	120	163	64	46	800	10	8	60	1.1	1.3	14	2.0	400	3.0	1200	1200	300	18	15	150
19–22	55	120	163	64	44	800	7.5	8	60	1.1	1.3	14	2.0	400	3.0	800	800	300	18	15	150
23–50	55	120	163	64	44	800	5	8	60	1.0	1.2	13	2.0	400	3.0	800	800	300	18	15	150
51+	55	120	163	64	44	800	5	8	60	1.0	1.2	13	2.0	400	3.0	800	800	300	10	15	150
Pregnant					+30	+200	+5	+2	+20	+0.4	+0.3	+2	+0.6	+400	+1.0	+400	+400	+150	h	+5	+25
Lactating					+20	+400	+5	+3	+40	+0.5	+0.5	+5	+0.5	+100	+1.0	+400	+400	+150	h	+10	+50

[a] Food and Nutrition Board, National Academy of Sciences—National Research Council (revised 1980). Designed for the maintenance of good nutrition of practically all healthy people in the United States. The allowances are intended to provide for individual variations among most normal persons as they live in the United States under usual environmental stresses. Diets should be based on a variety of common foods in order to provide other nutrients for which human requirements have been less well defined.

226

b Retinol equivalents. 1 retinol equivalent = 1 μg retinol or 6 μg beta carotene.

c As cholecalciferol, 10 μg cholecalciferol = 400 I.U. of vitamin D.

d α-tocopherol equivalents. 1 mg. d-α-tocopherol = α T.E.

e 1 NE (niacin equivalent) is equal to 1 mg. of niacin or 60 mg. of dietary tryptophan.

f The folacin allowances refer to dietary sources as determined by *Lactobacillus casei* assay after treatment with enzymes (conjugases) to make polyglutamyl forms of the vitamin available to the test organism.

g The recommended dietary allowance for vitamin B$_{12}$ in infants is based on average concentration of the vitamin in human milk. The allowances after weaning are based on energy intake (as recommended by the American Academy of Pediatrics) and consideration of other factors, such as intestinal absorption.

h The increased requirement during pregnancy cannot be met by the iron content of habitual American diets nor by the existing iron stores of many women; therefore the use of 30–60 mg. of supplemental iron is recommended. Iron needs during lactation are not substantially different from those of nonpregnant women, but continued supplementation of the mother for 2–3 months after parturition is advisable in order to replenish stores depleted by pregnancy.

ESTIMATED SAFE AND ADEQUATE DAILY DIETARY INTAKES OF ADDITIONAL SELECTED NUTRIENTS[a]

Age (years)	Vitamins			Trace elements						Electrolytes		
	Vitamin K (µg)	Biotin (µg)	Pantothenic acid (mg)	Copper (mg)	Manganese (mg)	Fluoride (mg)	Chromium (mg)	Selenium (mg)	Molybdenum (mg)	Sodium (mg)	Potassium (mg)	Chloride (mg)
0–0.5	12	35	2	0.5–0.7	0.5–0.7	0.1–0.5	0.01–0.04	0.01–0.04	0.03–0.06	115–350	350–925	275–700
0.5–1	10–20	50	3	0.7–1.0	0.7–1.0	0.2–1.0	0.02–0.06	0.02–0.06	0.04–0.08	250–750	425–1275	400–1200
1–3	15–30	65	3	1.0–1.5	1.0–1.5	0.5–1.5	0.02–0.08	0.02–0.08	0.05–0.1	325–975	550–1650	500–1500
4–6	20–40	85	3–4	1.5–2.0	1.5–2.0	1.0–2.5	0.03–0.12	0.03–0.12	0.06–0.15	450–1350	775–2325	700–2100
7–10	30–60	120	4–5	2.0–2.5	2.0–3.0	1.5–2.5	0.05–0.2	0.05–0.2	0.1 –0.3	600–1800	1000–3000	925–2775
11 +	50–100	100–200	4–7	2.0–3.0	2.5–5.0	1.5–2.5	0.05–0.2	0.05–0.2	0.15–0.5	900–2700	1525–4575	1400–4200
Adults	70–140	100–200	4–7	2.0–3.0	2.5–5.0	1.5–4.0	0.05–0.2	0.05–0.2	0.15–0.5	1100–3300	1875–5625	1700–5100

228

ENERGY ALLOWANCES[a]

Age (years)	Weight (kg)	Weight (lb)	Height (cm)	Height (in)	Energy needs[b] (cal)
Infants					
0.0–0.5	6	13	60	24	kg × 115 (95–145)
0.5–1.0	9	20	71	28	kg × 105 (80–135)
Children					
1–3	13	29	90	35	1300 (900–1800)
4–6	20	44	112	44	1700 (1300–2300)
7–10	28	62	132	52	2400 (1650–3300)
Males					
11–14	45	99	157	62	2700 (2000–3700)
15–18	66	145	176	69	2800 (2100–3900)
19–22	70	154	177	70	2900 (2500–3300)
23–50	70	154	178	70	2700 (2300–3100)
51–75	70	154	178	70	2400 (2000–2800)
76+	70	154	178	70	2050 (1650–2450)

Age (years)	Weight (kg)	Weight (lb)	Height (cm)	Height (in)	Energy needs[b] (cal)
Females					
11–14	46	101	157	62	2200 (1500–3000)
15–18	55	120	163	64	2100 (1200–3000)
19–22	55	120	163	64	2100 (1700–2500)
23–50	55	120	163	64	2000 (1600–2400)
51–75	55	120	163	64	1800 (1400–2200)
76+	55	120	163	64	1600 (1200–2000)
Pregnant					+300
Lactating					+500

[b] The energy allowances for the young adults are for men and women doing light work. The allowances for the two older age groups represent mean energy needs over these age spans, allowing for a 2% decrease in basal (resting) metabolic rate per decade and a reduction in activity of 200 cal per day for men and women between 51 and 75 years, 500 cal for men over 75 years, and 400 cal for women over 75. The customary range of daily energy output, shown in parentheses, is based on a variation in energy needs of 400 cal at any one age, emphasizing the wide range of energy intakes appropriate for any group of people. Energy allowances for children through age 18 are based on median energy intakes of children of these ages followed in longitudinal growth studies. The values in parentheses are tenth and ninetieth percentiles of energy intake, to indicate the range of energy consumption among children of these ages.

229

B. For Further Information

The following resources may be of interest to you in continuing your self-education on exercise and sports nutrition, general nutrition and weight control, healthy cooking, and New Age philosophy and self-help. For those resources unavailable in local bookstores, ordering information is provided.

EXERCISE AND SPORTS NUTRITION

Addleman, F. *The Winning Edge—Nutrition for Athletic Fitness and Performance*. Englewood Cliffs, NJ: Prentice Hall, 1984.

American Alliance for Health, Physical Education, Recreation, and Dance. *Nutrition for Sports Success*. AAHPERD, 1990 Association Drive, Reston, VA 20091, 1984.

American Heart Association. *Nutrition for the Fitness Challenge*. American Heart Association, 7320 Greenville Avenue, Dallas, TX 75231, 1983.

Anderson, B., and Anderson, J. *Stretching*. New York: Random House, 1980.

Barry, D. *Stay Fit and Healthy Until You're Dead*. Emmaus, PA: Rodale Press, 1985 (the lighter side of fitness).

Bicycling. Rodale Press, 33 E. Minor St., Emmaus, PA 18049 (a monthly magazine).

Canter, R. *Regaining Health and Fitness—Guided Exercises to Recover from Heart Attack, Lower Back Pain, Obesity, and Diabetes for Inactive Adults*. Brattleboro, VT: Stephen Green Press, 1982.

Coleman, E. *Eating for Endurance*. California Dietetic Association, Los Angeles District, PO Box 3506, Santa Monica, CA 90403, 1980.

Cooper, K., and Cooper, M. *The New Aerobics for Women*. New York: Bantam, 1988.

Corbin, C., and Lindsay, R. *The Ultimate Fitness Book*. Champaign, IL: Leisure Press, 1984.

Fixx, J. *The Complete Book of Running*. New York: Random House, 1977.

Garrick, J., and Radetsky, P. *Peak Condition—Winning Strategies to Prevent, Treat, and Rehabilitate Sports Injuries*. New York: Harper & Row, 1988.

Haxhausen, M., and Leman, R. *Body Sense*. New York: Pantheon Books, 1987.

Jerome, J. *Staying Supple—The Bountiful Pleasures of Stretching*. New York: Bantam, 1987.

Jonas, S. *Triathloning for Ordinary Mortals*. New York: W. W. Norton, 1986.

Jonas, S., and Radetsky, P. *PaceWalking: The Balanced Way to Aerobic Health*. New York: Crown Publishers, 1988.

Katz, J. *Swimming for Total Fitness*. Garden City, NY: Dolphin/Double-day, 1981.

McKee, G. *Nutrition and the Athlete*. Van Nuys, CA: PM, Inc., 1986.

Nieman, D., *The Sports Medicine Fitness Course*. Bull Publishing Co., PO Box 208, Palo Alto, CA 94302, 1986.

Prudden, B. *Bonnie Prudden's After Fifty Fitness Guide*. New York: Ballantine, 1986.

Runner's World. Rodale Press, 33 E. Minor Street, Emmaus, PA 18049 (a monthly magazine).

Running & Fit News. American Running & Fitness Association, 9310 Old Georgetown Road, Bethesda, MD 20814 (a monthly newsletter).

Shangold, M. *The Complete Sports Medicine Book for Women*. New York: Simon and Schuster, 1985.

Sports-Nutrition News. Healthmere Press, PO Box 986, Evanston, IL 60204 (a bimonthly newsletter).

Thomas, G., *et al. Exercise and Health*. Cambridge, MA: Oelgeschlager, Gunn and Hain, 1981.

Turock, A. *Getting Physical—How to Stick with Your Exercise Program*. New York: Doubleday, 1988.

Williams, M. *Nutrition for Fitness and Sport*. Dubuque, IA: William C. Brown Co., 1983.

Wilmore, J. *Sensible Fitness*. Champaign, IL: Leisure Press, 1986.

GENERAL NUTRITION AND WEIGHT CONTROL

American Heart Association. *Eating for a Healthy Heart*. American Heart Association, 7320 Greenville Avenue, Dallas, TX 75231, 1983.

American Institute for Cancer Research. *Planning Meals That Lower Cancer Risk*. AICR, PO Box 76216, Washington, DC 20013, 1984.

Aronson, V. *Thirty Days to Better Nutrition*. Englewood Cliffs, NJ: Prentice Hall College Division, 1987.

Aronson, V., and Stare, F. *Food for Today's Teens*. Philadelphia: George F. Stickley Publishing Co., 1985.

Baker, S., and Henry, R. *Parent's Guide to Nutrition*. Reading, MA: Addison-Wesley Publishing Co., 1987.

Berkeley Wellness Letter. PO Box 10922, Des Moines, IA 50340 (a monthly newsletter).

Brody, J. *Jane Brody's Nutrition Book*. New York: W. W. Norton, 1981.

Chernin, K. *The Hungry Self*. New York: Harper & Row, 1985.

Connor, S., and Connor, W. *The New American Diet*. New York: Simon and Schuster, 1986.

DeBakey, M. *The Living Heart Diet*. New York: Simon and Schuster, 1984.

Deutsch, R. *The Fat Counter Guide*. Bull Publishing Co., PO Box 208, Palo Alto, CA 94302, 1978.

Doress, P., and Siegal, D. *Ourselves, Growing Older*. New York: Simon and Schuster, 1987.

Environmental Nutrition. 2112 Broadway, Suite 200, New York, NY 10023 (a monthly newsletter).

Eisenberg, A.; Eisenberg-Murkoff, H.; Eisenberg-Hathaway, S. *What to Eat When You're Expecting*. New York: Workman Publishing, 1986.

Farquhar, J. *The American Way of Life Need Not Be Hazardous to Your Health*, 2nd edition. Reading, MA: Addison-Wesley, 1987.

Franz, M.; Hedding, B.; Leitch, G. *Opening the Door to Good Nutrition*. International Diabetes Center, 4959 Excelsior Boulevard, Minneapolis, MN 55416, 1985.

Goor, R., and Goor, N. *Eater's Choice—A Food Lover's Guide to Lower Cholesterol*. Boston: Houghton Mifflin, 1987.

Hamilton, E.; Whitney, E.; Sizer, F. *Nutrition—Concepts and Controversies*, 3rd edition. St. Paul, MN: West Publishing Co., 1985.

Hausman, P. *The Calcium Bible*. New York: Rawson Associates, 1985.

Jacobson, M., and Fritschner, S. *The Fast-Food Guide*. New York: Workman Publishing, 1986.

Lansky, V. *Fat-Proofing Your Children . . . So That They Never Become Diet-Addicted Adults*. New York: Bantam, 1988.

Long, P. *The Nutritional Ages of Women—A Lifetime Guide to Eating Right for Health, Beauty, and Well-Being*. New York: Macmillan, 1986.

Natow, A., and Heslin, J. *Nutrition for the Prime of Your Life*. New York: McGraw-Hill, 1983.

Reader's Digest. *Eat Better, Live Better*. Pleasantville, NY: Reader's Digest Association, 1982.

Saltman, P.; Gurin, J.; Mothner, I. *The California Nutrition Book*. Boston: Little, Brown, 1987.

Satter, E. *How to Get Your Kid to Eat . . . But Not Too Much*. Bull Publishing Co., PO Box 208, Palo Alto, CA 94302, 1987.

Schwartz, H. *Never Satisfied—A Cultural History of Diets, Fantasies, and Fat*. New York: Macmillan/The Free Press, 1986.

Stern, B. *The Food Book—The Complete Guide to the Most Popular Brand Name Foods in the U.S.* New York: Dell, 1987.

Tufts University Diet and Nutrition Letter. PO Box 10948, Des Moines, IA 50940 (a monthly newsletter).

U.S. Department of Agriculture. *Nutrition and Your Health—Dietary Guidelines for Americans*, 2nd edition. Superintendent of Documents, U.S. Government Printing Office, Washington, DC 20402, 1985.

U.S. Department of Agriculture. *Nutritive Value of Foods*. Superintendent of Documents, U.S. Government Printing Office, Washington, DC 20402, 1985.

U.S. Surgeon General's Report on Nutrition and Health. Superintendent of Documents, U.S. Government Printing Office, Washington, DC 20402, 1988.

Winick, M. *For Mothers and Daughters—A Guide to Good Nutrition for Women*. New York: Berkley Books, 1983.

COOKBOOKS

American Cancer Society. *The Good Book of Nutrition*. American Cancer Society, Florida Division, 1001 S. MacDill Avenue, Tampa, FL 33629, 1987.

American Diabetes Association. *American Diabetes Association Family Cookbook*. Englewood Cliffs, NJ: Prentice Hall, 1984.

American Diabetes Association. *Holiday Cookbook*. Englewood Cliffs, NJ: Prentice Hall, Inc., 1986.

American Dietetic Association. *Dietitians' Food Favorites*. American Dietetic Association, 216 W. Jackson Boulevard, Chicago, IL 60606, 1986.

American Heart Association. *American Heart Association Cookbook*. New York: Ballantine, 1986.

American Institute for Cancer Research. *An Ounce of Prevention—Seasonal Cookbook Series*. AICR, PO Box 76216, Washington, DC 20013, 1986.

Artaud-Wild, S. *Simply Nutritious!* American Cancer Society, Oregon Division, Inc., 0330 SW Curry Street, Portland, OR 97201, 1986.

Brody, J. *Jane Brody's Good Food Book.* New York: W. W. Norton, 1985.

Burrows-Grad, L. *Make It Easy, Make It Light.* New York: Simon and Schuster, 1987.

Cooley, D., and Moore, C. *Eat Smart for a Healthy Heart Cookbook.* Woodbury, CT: Barron's, 1987.

Egan, J. *Healthy High-Fiber Cooking.* Tucson, AZ: HP Books, 1987.

Eisenberg, A.; Eisenberg, H.; Eisenberg, S. *The Special Guest Cookbook.* New York: Beaufort Books, 1982.

Gillard, J., and Kirkpatrick, J. *The Guiltless Gourmet.* Diabetes Center, Inc., PO Box 739, Wayzata, MN 55391, 1987.

Harsila, J., and Hansen, E. *Seafood—A Collection of Heart Healthy Recipes.* Richmond Beach, WA: National Seafood Educators, 1986.

Lindsay, A. *The American Cancer Society Cookbook.* New York: Hearst Books, 1988.

Marks, B. *The High-Calcium Low-Calorie Cookbook.* Chicago: Contemporary Books, 1987.

Metropolitan Life Insurance Co. *Eat Well, Be Well Cookbook.* New York: Simon and Schuster, 1986.

Robertson, L.; Flinders, C.; Godfrey, B. *The New Laurel's Kitchen.* Berkeley, CA: Ten Speed Press, 1986.

Rombauer, I., and Becker, M. *The Joy of Cooking.* New York: Macmillan, 1986 (the cook's bible, although recipes are *not* low-fat).

Roth, H. *Deliciously Low.* New York: New American Library, 1983.

——————. *Deliciously Simple.* New York: New American Library, 1986.

Schneider, E. *Uncommon Fruits and Vegetables—A Common Sense Guide.* New York: Harper & Row, 1987.

Shulman, M. R. *Gourmet Vegetarian Feasts.* Rochester, VT: Thorsen's Publishers, Inc., 1987.

Thomas, A. *The Vegetarian Epicure Book Two.* New York: Alfred A. Knopf, 1987.

Underwood, G. *Gourmet Light.* Chester, CT: The Globe Pequot Press, 1985.

——————. *The Enlightened Gourmet.* Chester, CT: The Globe Pequot Press, 1987.

Vegetarian Times. *Vegetarian Times Cookbook.* New York: Macmillan, 1984.

Zukin, J. *Milk-Free Diet Cookbook—Cooking for the Lactose Intolerant.* New York: Sterling Publishing Co., 1982.

NEW AGE SELF-HELP

Achterberg, J. *Imagery and Healing.* Boston: Shambala Press, 1985.

Benson, H. *Your Maximum Mind.* New York: Times Books, 1987.

Borysenko, J. *Minding the Body, Mending the Mind.* Reading, MA: Addison-Wesley, 1987.

Eliot, R., and Breo, D. *Is It Worth Dying For?* New York: Bantam, 1984.
Ferguson, M. *The Aquarian Conspiracy.* New York: St. Martin's Press, 1980.
Ferguson, M., ed. *Brain/Mind Bulletin,* Box 42211, Los Angeles, CA 90004 (a newsletter).
Forman, J., and Meyers, D. *The Personal Stress Reduction Program.* Englewood Cliffs, NJ: Prentice Hall, 1987.
Gawain, S. *Creative Visualization.* New York: Bantam, 1978.
Gendlin, E. *Focusing.* New York: Bantam, 1981.
Hutchinson, M. *Transforming Body Image.* Trumansburg, NY: The Crossing Press, 1985.
Levine, S. *A Gradual Awakening.* New York: Anchor Press/Doubleday, 1979.
—————. *Healing into Life and Death.* New York: Anchor Press/Doubleday, 1987.
Metzner, R. *Opening to Inner Light.* New York: St. Martin's Press, 1986.
Mind Body Health Digest and *Advances.* Institute for the Advancement of Health, 16 E. 53rd Street, New York, NY 10022 (quarterly publications).
New Age Journal. Rising Star Association, 342 Western Avenue, Brighton, MA 02135 (a bimonthly magazine).
Pearsall, P. *Superimmunity.* New York: Fawcett, 1987.
Peck, M. S. *The Road Less Traveled.* New York: Simon and Schuster, 1985.
Rice, P. *Stress and Health.* Monterey, CA: Brooks/Cole Publishing Co., 1987.
Roberts, J. *The Nature of Personal Reality.* New York: Bantam, 1987.
Selye, H. *Stress without Distress.* Philadelphia: Lippincott, 1974.
Siegal, B. *Love, Medicine & Miracles.* New York: Harper & Row, 1986.
Williams, S. *The Practice of Personal Transformation.* Berkeley, CA: Journey Press, 1985.
Witkin, G. *Quick Fixes and Small Comforts—How Every Woman Can Resist Those Irresistable Urges.* New York: Villard, 1988.

RESOURCE CENTERS AND WALKING CLUBS

American College of Sports Medicine, PO Box 1440, Indianapolis, IN 46206.
American Dietetic Association, 216 W. Jackson Boulevard, Chicago, IL 60606.
American Heart Association, 7320 Greenville Avenue, Dallas, TX 75231.
American Running & Fitness Association, 9310 Old Georgetown Road, Bethesda, MD 20814.
American Walkers Association, 6221 Robison Road, Cincinnati, OH 45213.

Food and Nutrition Information and Education Resources Center, National Agricultural Library, Room 304, Beltsville, MD 20705.

Institute for the Advancement of Health, 16 E. 53rd Street, New York, NY 10022.

National Self-Help Clearing House, 33 W. 42nd Street, New York, NY 10036.

PaceWalkers of America®, Inc. Box QQ, East Setauket, NY 11733 (Dr. Jonas's organization).

Prevention Magazine Walking Club, 33 E. Minor Street, Emmaus, PA 18049.

Walkers Club of America, Box M, Livingston Manor, NY 12758.

The WalkWays Center, Suite 427, 783 15th Street, Washington, DC 20005.

Index

Index

Bulb baster, 182
Bulgur, 183
Bulgur wheat, 182
B vitamins, 205–7

C

Caffeine, sources of, 210–12
Calcium, 194, 202–5
  foods high in, 203–4
Calcium blockers, 205
Calcium robbers, 205
Calisthenics, 64
Caloric balance theory, 7
Calories, 8
Cambridge diet, 11
Cancer, 214
Carbohydrate loading diets, 89
Carbohydrates, 105
Carob, 184
Cellulite, 64–65
Cereal choices, fiber-rich, 126
Cheese, 185–87
  fats in, 185–87
Cholesterol, 141–42
  reading label for, 174
Cholesterol-rich foods
  high-fat, 141
  low-fat, 142
Clothing, for PaceWalking, 62–63
Cocoa powder, 183
Complementary foods, 103, 106
  in IDEAL eating plan, 117, 122, 128
Complex carbohydrates, 106, 142
Convenience foods, fats in, 162–63
Cookbook selection, 189–90
Cooper, Kenneth, 71, 76
Couscous, 183
Creative cooking, 182–85
Cruciferous vegetables, 214

D

Dehydration, prevention of, 89–90
Desserts, preparing, 183
Diaphragm, 69
Dietary Guidelines for Americans, 138, 142, 151
Diet foods, 131–32
Diets
  carbohydrate loading, 89
  fad, 9–14, 103
  low-calorie, 8–9, 11, 138–39
  popular, 10–11
Diet trap, getting out of the, 7–24
Digital stop watch, 63
Dining Out: A Guide to Restaurant Dining, 166
Dinner, in IDEAL eating plan, 119, 124, 129–30
Distress, eustress versus, 38
Doctor, consulting your, 54–55
Dr. Atkins' diet, 11
Dr. Stillman's diet, 11

E

Eating cues
  emotional, 35–36
  environmental, 34–35
Eating habits, 25–26, 220
  accepting your unique physique, 45–47
  attitude toward, 27, 29–30
  changing, 120–21, 126, 131
  eustress vs. distress, 38
  and fat slashing, 120–21, 125, 130–31
  fear of failure, 41–42
  fear of success, 41–42
  importance of, 103–4
  moral support, 39–41
  and motivation, 32–33

250 · *Index*